Invitation to Philosophy

Invitation to Philosophy

Imagined Dialogues
with Great Philosophers

by
YUVAL STEINITZ

Translated from the Hebrew by
Naomi Goldblum

Hackett Publishing Company, Inc.
Indianapolis/Cambridge

13 12 11 10 09 08   2 3 4 5 6 7 8

For further information, please address
    Hackett Publishing Company, Inc.
    P. O. Box 44937
    Indianapolis, IN 46244-0937
    www.hackettpublishing.com

Text design by Dan Kirklin

Library of Congress Cataloging-in-Publication Data

Steinitz, Yuval, 1958–
    [Hazmanah le-filosofyah.   English]
    An invitation to philosophy/Yuval Steinitz: translated from the
Hebrew by Naomi Goldblum.
        p.   cm.
    Includes index.
    ISBN 0-87220-266-6 (alk. paper).   ISBN 0-87220-265-8 (pbk.: alk.
paper).
    1. Philosophy—Introductions.   2. Imaginary conversations.
I. Title.
BD28.S7513   1994   94-22596
100—dc20   CIP

ISBN-13: 978-0-87220-266-5 (cloth)
ISBN-13: 978-0-87220-265-8 (pbk.)

The paper used in this publication meets the minimum requirements
of American National Standard for Information Sciences—
Permanence of Paper for Printed Library Materials, ANSI Z39.48–1984.
∞

Contents

A Bevy of Thanks

I thank Yeshayahu Leibowitz for his help and encouragement, as well as for his suggestion that I include a chapter on Kant; Devora Kamert for poring over the typescript and offering many thoughtful comments; and Menachem Brinker for his helpful comments.

I also wish to thank David Zilka, Nathan Rotenstreich, and Eliahu Rosenow for their help and support.

I am most grateful to my friends and relatives whose unrelenting criticism throughout the writing couldn't have been more effective: Gila Canfi, who is now my wife; my sisters Talia Arad, Mikhal Steinitz, and Shira Steinitz; Amnon Horowitz; and my parents, Mina and Dan, who devoted many hours to proofreading the text.

Thanks also go to those who helped with the English translation: Naomi Goldblum, who managed to translate, and in places even improve, the problematic text of a problematic author; and the poet Aluma Halter, who contributed helpful suggestions.

Finally, I am happy to mention my students at the Hebrew University of Jerusalem and its attached high school. Their enthusiasm for philosophy served as an inspiration for my writing *Invitation to Philosophy*.

Y.S.

Preface

In 1983 I was asked to teach a "very introductory" course in philosophy at the Youth Science Center attached to the Hebrew University of Jerusalem.

Having decided on the topics I wanted to discuss, I looked for suitable texts from which to teach them. At this stage I ran into a problem: Many of the classical texts in philosophy are quite complex and difficult, and coming to grips with them would have demanded a great deal of my students' time (as well as close individual supervision on my part).

To overcome this difficulty, I chose a few excellent modern introductions to philosophy. In particular, we concentrated on Russell's *The Problems of Philosophy*, which deals extensively with epistemology, and R. Taylor's *Metaphysics*, which covers a variety of topics.

But there were two problems with this decision. First, although these introductions were very clear, they were written very authoritatively. Second, the thoughts of the philosophers they dealt with were not presented directly, which left the reader in ignorance of the philosophers' individual styles of reasoning and of writing. I was therefore pleased to accept the suggestion of David Zilka, the department head, to compile a booklet suitable for use in introductory philosophy courses.

I had intended to base the booklet on excerpts from the classical texts, prefacing each text with an explanatory note to make it easier for the students to understand. However, when I sat down to write, something weird and wonderful occurred: the original source material and the explanatory passages got mixed up and merged into one another in my mind. This book consists of the product of this process of amalgamation.

*

The book is written mainly in dialogue form. In most of the chapters a conversation takes place among a number of characters, one of whom is the protagonist, who sets forth his view (usually a very definite view) of the topic under discussion. Some of the speakers are well-known philosophers, and they present their views and arguments in a form closely corresponding to the original style of their writing. The other speakers are imaginary characters who were created to challenge the protagonist.

The book consists of three parts. The first addresses problems of epistemology, asking questions such as: Is the truth discoverable? Do we acquire our knowledge of the world through our five senses, or by way of pure thought? The ideas of several important philosophers are presented: the ancient Greeks Parmenides and Zeno, and the modern philosophers Descartes, Hume, and Kant.

The second part presents the soul-body or mind-body problem, focusing on the questions: Who am I? Am I a body? Am I perhaps a soul? Or could I be a combination of body and soul coexisting in the same being? Here the materialist and the dualist converse with a neutral truth-seeker. This part ends with a presentation of the ideas of the eighteenth-century philosopher George Berkeley.

The third part of the book deals with the subject of free will and determinism. Determinism holds that everything that happens in the world is preordained, and therefore negates the existence of free will and true liberty. Two sections present the problem from different angles. In the first a conversation takes place between a determinist and libertarian. The second is a mock-Socratic dialogue which keeps as faithfully as possible to the general spirit of Socrates' own ideas on this subject.

Since the book is intended for students with a limited background in philosophy, as well as for readers who may have no philosophical background at all, I have added an appendix to each part, referring the reader to additional material dealing with the topic under discussion. I have chosen essays and passages that have had great influence on the history of philosophical thought, yet which are nevertheless not too difficult for the beginner.

Finally, a few words about the selection of subjects for discussion: This book does not pretend to cover all the problems dealt with in the entire field of philosophical inquiry. Those chosen to be presented are those which engaged my students and me in a course whose primary purpose was to arouse an initial interest in philosophy. This I tried to achieve by means of philosophical theories which seemed to possess a relatively high factor of provocation, perhaps even irritation.

For there is no better way to arouse interest and involvement in philosophy than by annoying your listeners and readers. In this way you undermine their complacency and involve them emotionally.

What Is Philosophy?

"What is philosophy?" is itself a philosophical problem.

Is the question "What is physics?" also a problem in physics? Not at all. Research in physics cannot provide an answer to this question, as there is no physical answer to it. Similarly, the question "What is agriculture?" has no answer in "agricultural" terms. The same is true of questions like "What is music?" and "What is art?" Even the honorable question "What is the essence of science?" or "What should be called 'science'?" does not have a scientific answer.

This short discussion already gives us a kind of characterization of philosophy—that, among other things, it reflects upon itself.

Questions like "What is science?" and "What is art?" and "What is the difference between the rational and the empirical sciences?" are first and foremost questions of a philosophical nature.

What then is philosophy? What distinguishes it from physics, algebra, art, poetry, agriculture, psychology, and astronomy? What are the essential features of philosophy that can be used to define it?

The most characteristic feature of philosophy is its comprehensiveness. Each of the other sciences and disciplines relates principally to a specific aspect of reality—physical, psychological, visual, and so on. This aspect is determined by the basic methods used in the particular science or art. And philosophy? Philosophy deals with everything.

Does the assertion that "philosophy deals with everything" mean that every question that can be raised is actually a philosophical question? Are questions about the number of Julius Caesar's soldiers, or about the intensity of the ultraviolet emission from the sun, philosophical questions? If this were the case, it would follow that philosophy is equal to the sum of all the sciences and arts taken together: Philosophy = physics

+ biology + literature + history + astronomy + ... Obviously this is not the case.

Questions like the ones cited above, as well as an enormous number of additional questions, are far from being philosophical. It is possible, of course, to link any question whatsoever to some philosophical issue. But in principle most of the questions we ask, in our daily lives or in our academic work, are not genuinely philosophical questions.

When we say "Philosophy deals with everything," we do not claim that philosophy refers to each and every particular subject separately. We claim that it deals with one important thing: *everything*.

What, then, distinguishes philosophy from the various fields we have mentioned? While each of them relates to a particular aspect (or aspects) of reality, the subject of philosophy is *"everything,"* or the totality of things. Philosophy wonders about, and tries to solve, the most comprehensive puzzles: What is the world? What is it made of? Who and what am I? What is knowledge, and can we ever be certain that we have it? What is a good question and what can be considered a good answer? What is reason, and what are its rules? Can this last question be answered by psychology? Who created the world? And why? What can be known, and what cannot?

Since philosophy is the common denominator of all human thought, and since it raises the most general questions, it naturally tries to avoid, or at least minimize, dealing with particular questions. Thus, whenever it becomes possible to offer specific answers to a given question by using a particular empirical procedure, this question is removed from the realm of philosophy and becomes a scientific issue.

*

What is the use of philosophy? Well, we know that people generally do things for some purpose. The purpose of agriculture, for instance, is to provide us with food; of industry, to provide us with goods; of medicine, to lengthen our lives; and philosophy . . . ?

Doing philosophy is not practical in the sense of "doing

something in order to achieve something else." From this perspective it may be compared to music. Why do we make music? Why do we listen to it? It does not improve our standard of living; it does not provide us with food, goods, or health. We listen to music *for its own sake,* and we do philosophy for its own sake. Both music and philosophy are ends in themselves; they are not meant to achieve other goals. In a certain sense they are "final purposes": We occupy ourselves with the sciences and with various types of work in order to improve and lengthen our lives. But what do we live for? To occupy ourselves with final goals: art, music, and philosophy.

And doesn't philosophy contribute anything to our practical life?

If it doesn't, then it would seem that there is some point to all the arguments we hear in times of economic difficulty—that the government must stop subsidizing the study of philosophy and the arts and dedicate this money to the more practical fields of scientific research. But the issue is not so simple.

Take physics, for example: in contemporary research a distinction is made between theoretical physics and applied physics. In the past, when scientists engaged in theoretical studies, it was sometimes argued that their work was not practical and that they ought to devote their talents to the practical problems of physics, chemistry, and mathematics that are directly relevant to technological progress.

Nowadays people are more aware of the fact that theoretical research affects both practical research and technology, and that the difference between applied physics and theoretical physics is that the practical results of theoretical physics are obtained only after many years, whereas the effect of applied physics on industrial technology is evident within a few years or even months.

But this is true of philosophy as well. In much the same way that theoretical physics eventually affects and influences applied physics and technology, philosophy influences theoretical physics. The philosophy of science, for example, is a theoretical area dealing with scientific methods and theories—a sort of theory of theories. This hierarchical scheme yields the following chain of influence:

Philosophy
↓
Theoretical Physics
↓
Applied Physics
↓
Technology

It takes quite a long time for the influence of theoretical physics to reach technology, and even longer for a theory or a new perspective in philosophy to demonstrate its relevance to technology and our way of life. Nevertheless, this influence does exist and is quite effectual; we need only remember that all our present-day sciences grew out of the study of philosophy.

Since it takes an inordinate amount of time for the practical influences of philosophy to be felt, the philosopher is liberated from the heavy chains that bind most scientists and researchers— the realization of "practical uses" for their thought and activities. This liberation is another important feature of the special character of philosophy.

PART I
EPISTEMOLOGY

Epistemology is a central area in philosophy. Its leading questions are: How is it possible to know the world? Do we come to know it through our five senses? Is empirical science—constructing theories by analyzing the data provided by the senses—the highway to reality and truth?

Some philosophers have vigorously denied the common view that it is possible to know the world through the senses and through scientific research. Their arguments cannot be lightly brushed aside. We will see this for ourselves in our encounter with the theories of Parmenides and Zeno, who lived in ancient Greece, and David Hume, an eighteenth-century Scot.

Hume cast doubt on the reliability of the scientific method of induction, while Parmenides, besides casting doubt on learning from experience, suggested an alternative method through which knowing the world would be possible. "What is the world?" asked Parmenides, and he answered: "The world is exactly 'what there is' or 'the truth.'" And how is it possible to encounter "the truth," i.e., to come to know "what there is"? "Through rational philosophical thought," was Parmenides' answer.

A somewhat similar approach was taken by the seventeenth-century French philosopher René Descartes, whose first question was "How can I attain an absolutely certain truth?" Descartes, too, believed that such a truth can be attained only through philosophical reasoning (and not through the senses or science), although his reasoning led him to an entirely different solution from that of Parmenides.

Parmenides, Zeno, and Descartes belong to the Rationalist stream in philosophy, which stresses the role of pure intellect and philosophical thinking and reduces (or sometimes even totally denies) the role of the senses and the empirical sciences. (A central figure in the establishment of the rationalist approach was Plato, but we will not present his epistemology here.)

An empiricist philosopher whose theory is directly relevant to

5

the problems of epistemology was George Berkeley, who appears in this book in Part II. Berkeley believed that we come to know the world through our senses. Moreover, he claimed that "to exist is to be perceived," meaning that "the unobservable" does not exist at all.

Hume, whom we have already mentioned, also starts out from the common assumption that our sense perceptions are our sole means for coming to know the world. The principal concept he examined in this context is the concept of "causality." The result of this examination, however, was extremely puzzling: the accepted picture of science collapsed like a house of cards and buried pure empiricism under its ruins. Hume's role among his empiricist colleagues may be compared to that of Samson, who brought down the Philistine temple on himself as well as on the Philistines.

Finally, we will present a minute sample of the ideas of Immanuel Kant, an eighteenth-century German philosopher who attempted to rebuild the ruins of the temple of science by solving the extremely difficult problems posed by Hume. To this end he invented an extensive and sophisticated theory. Many philosophers consider Kant's theory to be a blend of rationalism and empiricism, a theory which validates science on the basis of purely philosophical reasons. This theory even claims that we know the world partly through our "pure reason," though it considers the data gathered through the senses to be the raw material without which the generation of any world-picture would be impossible.

1

Parmenides:
'' 'What Is' Exists and the Nothing Does Not Exist''

No one knows when Parmenides was born or died, but it is generally agreed that he developed his ideas in the fifth century B.C. Parmenides was an extremely unusual phenomenon not only in Greek philosophy but in the general history of ideas as well. His basic premise was that '' 'what is' exists and the nothing does not exist.'' Could anyone deny this trivial assertion? Isn't it simply a tautology? Do we require a philosopher to tell us that *what is exists and the nothing does not exist*? Isn't it obvious not only to every mature adult but even to toddlers who have just learned to talk? For how could it be possible for the existent not to exist? That is, for *"what there is" not to be*? If it is absent, then obviously it is not what there is. And on the other hand, could it be possible for *the nothing to exist*? If it existed, then it would be something and not nothing.

This strange philosopher claimed that he wrote down what one of the Greek goddesses whispered in his ear:

Come, then, hear my dictum, and preserve it word by word:
What are the two paths of inquiry that can be thought of?
The one is "what is" and mustn't be absent;
It is the straight path that encounters truth.

The other is "what is not," which is consigned to the void;
This path, I warn you, you must always avoid;
For you cannot encounter what there is not.
Thus it can't be referred to, or even thought.

There is only one thing to say about the nothing: that it does not exist. Besides that, there's nothing to be found out or said about it. Therefore, in order to investigate the essence of the world, we must take the high road to 'what is.'

But we have already said that it exists; is there anything else that can be said about it with the same certainty? Are there other propositions about 'what there is' that can be directly confirmed by logic and pure reason, without our judgment being based on empirical investigation, sense perceptions, and the like?

"Of course," answered Parmenides. For example:

"It was never created."

For if the existent had ever been created, then one of two possibilities must have occurred: Either it was created from something, or it was created from nothing. But if 'what there is' was created from something, then it already existed, so it was not newly created. And how could it have been created from nothing? Don't we agree with Shakespeare that "nothing will come of nothing"?

"It will never disappear."

For if it will disappear into "what there is," then it will still exist—and so it will not have disappeared. And how could it disappear into the nothing? We have already agreed that the nothing does not exist . . .

> Thus "what there is" exists forever;
> It was not created, and will perish never.

This is the type of argument and proof used by Parmenides. Of course it provoked a good many thinkers to argue against it. But to this very day—more than 2400 years later—no one has succeeded in pointing out any clear logical flaw in his reasoning.

What else did Parmenides prove this way?

"It is perfect and fills all of space."

For how could it not fill all of space? If it did not, then we would have to admit that there is an empty space in at least one certain place. This is equivalent to saying that "in that certain place there is no 'what is,' but only nothing." But if we maintain our initial agreement that "what is" exists by definition, then we cannot say that in a certain place there is no "what there is"—for what there is cannot be absent. Likewise, we cannot say that there is nothing in that place, since we have already agreed that the phrase "there is nothing" is self-contradictory. "Nothing" cannot exist and cannot fill any space.

It thus turns out that the entire world is completely filled with what there is, and emptiness is eliminated.

"It is of uniform density."

For how could density be less in one place and greater in another? If it were unevenly distributed, this would mean that in one place there would be less of "what there is" in the same amount of space. And what could there be in that part of space that is not filled up by "what there is"? The only two possibilities are something and nothing. If something is there, then after all "what there is" *does* fill everything completely, and the density is the same in all places. And could there be nothing there? This would be self-contradictory; the nothing does not exist, and so it cannot occupy any space.

"It is in absolute rest."

> Since "what there is" is the entire world,
> It has no center, nor any end;
> Motionless it stays in its place
> Unaltered and unchanged.
>
> For how could it evoke an act
> When it has no void nor any part?
> And where could it go apace
> If there is no empty space?

The ordinary world-picture   Parmenides' world-picture

The impossibility of motion in Parmenides' world may be illustrated by the children's game in which numbers must be moved around within a rigid framework until they are all in numerical order.

The Parmenidean world-picture can only be grasped abstractly. Yet despite its oddity we will attempt to illustrate it with the help of another oddity: the astronomical phenomenon known as the "black hole."

What are black holes?

They are stars whose mass is several times greater than that of our sun. Such a great mass generates an enormous gravitational force, which also acts on the star itself. Therefore, at a certain stage in its life cycle the star begins to collapse toward its center, until it has only a very small volume—for example, a star with a mass three times that of our sun will end up with a radius of only ten kilometers.

The density of matter in such a star is enormous, so that the elementary particles actually "touch" and "press upon" one another. There is no motion there, because there are no empty spaces to move to. And since its gravitational force is so strong and concentrated, no particle can escape from the star to interstellar space. Any particle—such as a proton or a photon (a light particle)—that attempts to break away from the star will immediately be recaptured, just as a stone thrown above the surface of the earth will eventually stop rising and fall back to the surface. That's why such a star is called a black hole—no light is able to radiate away from it for us to see.

Within a black hole nothing moves and nothing changes. It is a frozen world, absolutely lifeless and uniform in its composition, as if time had come to a standstill.

But what does this have to do with Parmenides?

Since his world is filled with "what there is" at maximal density, the picture we get is similar to that of a black hole. It is filled with uniform "what is" of infinite density, without any movement or happening—just like a star that has evolved into a black hole.

And if there is no movement, then there will never be any change. For how could anything change without any motion? The world is therefore lifeless and frozen; it is in exactly the same state that it was a minute ago, a year ago, even a thousand years ago. And it will stay this way forever, since it cannot be altered. "There is nothing new under the sun," says Ecclesiastes; there is nothing new, there never was anything new, and there never will be anything new—and there is no sun, says Parmenides.

There is no sun?

Of course there isn't! For there are no individual objects, in Parmenides' view. After all, what could the boundary between two distinct objects be made of? What could it look like, when all of space is totally filled by "what there is"? How could one thing be distinguished from another, if all parts of "what there is" (that is, the world) are completely dense, frozen, and motionless—all to the same extent?

We can summarize Parmenides' views thus:

There is only "what is."
Never created and will never cease.
Perfect, homogeneous and dense,
Indivisible and thus motionless.
Therefore keep in mind:
It must be One of its kind.

*

It is highly probable that arguments of the following sort were presented against Parmenides:

Can't you see that the world is made up of separate entities? That it is full of motion? That there are mountains, rivers, and trees? That everything moves and flows—some people die and others are born? That carts travel, and birds fly? That clouds release rain, and the seasons go by? Don't you feel, see, hear, and sense all this tumult of happenings?

Some more sophisticated arguments of the following sort have also been raised:

If this is true, then how can you be talking to us? Don't you feel that you're moving your lips while claiming that movement is impossible? And if everything in the world is one indivisible unity, then why do you speak to us as if we and you are different persons? And how do you dare to tell us about your new book in philosophy, while claiming that there can never be anything new?

How can these arguments be answered?

To this end Parmenides distinguished between the "way of appearance" and the "way of truth." The "way of appearance" denotes whatever can be discovered through the five senses—vision, hearing, touch, taste, and smell. All the arguments presented above by his opponents were of this type: Don't you *see* this or that? Don't you *hear*? *Smell* and *taste*? *Touch* and *feel*?

In contrast, the "way of truth" denotes everything people can know without using their senses—without observing the world around them. These are propositions like "1 + 1 = 2" and "Parallel lines never meet," or even "There is only what is" and "The nothing does not exist."

Modern philosophy makes the same distinction using somewhat different words. "The way of appearance" is analogous to the "empirical sciences"—that is, the sciences based on observation and experiment: geology, physics, chemistry, astronomy, biology, etc. In all these sciences we use our bodily senses to find out about the world. (Sometimes we use instruments, as when we look at the world through a microscope or a telescope; but observation *through* an instrument is still sensory observation.) "The way of truth" is analogous to the "rational sciences"—that is, the sciences based on pure reason alone: arithmetic, geometry, logic, and, after Parmenides, philosophy too. People have never needed laboratories for these sciences. Teachers do not require labs to teach geometry or arithmetic.

My arguments, says Parmenides, emerge from "the way of truth"; that is, they are arguments of logic.

Parmenides freely admits that these logical arguments together with their fantastic conclusions are incompatible with common sense and the natural sciences. But in his opinion, whenever logic conflicts with the senses, or with the sciences based on them, we must put our trust in logic. For the senses are apt to deceive us, but logic can never lead to error.

If we translate this argument into modern terminology, Parmenides would argue, for instance, that mathematics is far more reliable and certain than chemistry or astronomy. Mathematics teaches us that $2 + 2 = 4$; and even if it seems to us, under certain circumstances, that $2 + 2 = 5$, we should not be tempted to abandon our faith in mathematics. Rather, we would assume that we were dreaming or hallucinating, or that someone was deceiving us, as magicians often do.

Thus Parmenides answers his critics: "You are coming to me in the name of the senses, but I am coming to you in the name of logic! You shouldn't consider the so-called evidence of the senses when logic teaches you otherwise, because logic, and only logic, is 'the way of truth.' "

2
Zeno:
Achilles and the Tortoise

Parmenides had a pupil named Zeno. Seeing that most people mocked his master's views, and that many philosophers and scholars claimed that he must have made some error, Zeno attempted to defend his master's fantastic theory.

The issue on which Parmenides was apparently attacked most often was the impossibility of motion. As far as other issues were concerned, such as the claim that the world is full of "what there is," people could easily reconcile it with their ordinary perception by assuming that what seemed empty to them was actually full of air or some other invisible substance. Even regarding the impossibility of "what there is" (which is no less than the entire world) having been created, no one could consider arguing that he had actually seen the creation of the world. But motion is different; anyone could claim that he saw motion with his own eyes.

In order to defend Parmenides' theory against this sort of argument (as well as other arguments), Zeno developed a new defense technique—reductio ad absurdum.

Zeno said to the critics: "You claim that motion exists? Well and good. Let's agree that the senses may be trusted, and stipulate that motion exists. Then we'll see what conclusions might follow."

The paradox of Achilles and the Tortoise
Achilles was the swiftest runner among the legendary heroes of the Trojan War; the Greeks called him "Achilles the fleet-footed."

The Tortoise, on the other hand, is a symbol of slowness.

"Let's assume," said Zeno, "that Achilles and the Tortoise are having a race. Since Achilles is the swifter runner, it would be only fair to give Mr. Tortoise a handicap of, say, ten meters, as the length of the entire track is 100 meters." (See the diagram.)

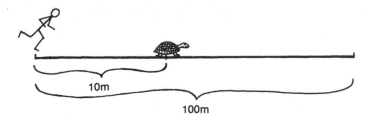

Achilles and the Tortoise at the start of the race

"And who do you think will win?" asks Zeno.

"Obviously Achilles will beat the Tortoise," answer Parmenides' opponents, who rely on the senses.

"But in order to win the race, doesn't Achilles have to overtake the Tortoise?" asks Zeno.

"Certainly," answer his opponents.

"Listen carefully," says Zeno. "Achilles will never even catch up with the Tortoise."

"What?"

"Let's say Achilles runs ten times faster than Mr. Tortoise," says Zeno. "Then when he has passed the first ten meters and has reached the spot where the Tortoise started out, the Tortoise will have passed one meter, won't he?"

"Correct."

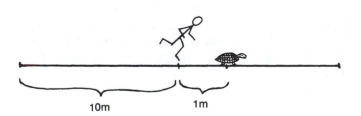

One second later: The gap narrows but never disappears
completely

"Now, in order for Achilles to reach the Tortoise," Zeno goes on, "he has to pass this extra meter as well, doesn't he?"

"Obviously."

"But while Achilles is zooming through this tiny distance, the

Tortoise is also continuing to move ahead, and during this time he will gain ten centimeters.''

"True."

"Well, then, he still hasn't caught up with the Tortoise," asserts Zeno.

"Okay, but now the distance between them has been narrowed to ten centimeters," say his opponents.

"True," replies Zeno, "but in order to catch up with the Tortoise, Achilles must pass these ten centimeters too. And while he's doing this the Tortoise will progress another little bit, won't he?"

"Yes," they admit.

"Therefore," Zeno concludes, "Achilles will never catch up with the Tortoise, as each time Achilles travels the remaining distance between his own position and that of the Tortoise, the Tortoise will also make some progress, and won't be waiting in the same spot anymore.

"Don't you see? In order to win the race Achilles has to overtake the Tortoise; yet in order to overtake it, he must first catch up with it. Yet in order to catch up with it he must first close the gap between their positions. And how can this be done, if every time the initial gap is closed, the Tortoise opens up a new one?"

*

One of the opponents found a tortoise at the side of the road. Quickly he placed it on the path a few meters ahead of him and shouted to Zeno: "Look here, Zeno—let's see who's right. That tree over there''—he pointed to a tree at the end of the path—"will be the finish line of the race that the tortoise and I are now starting."

The man began running energetically and quickly reached the end of the track.

"You see, Zeno," said the others, laughing, "it really is possible to catch up with tortoises."

"Well," said Zeno, "obviously we *see* that the tortoise was beaten in the race. But when we *think* about it, it seems that our sight must be deceiving us, since what we just saw is logically impossible. Or can one of you perhaps resolve this paradox?"

There was a moment of silence. Finally one of them said, "Even if it is valid, your paradox proves only that a faster thing cannot overtake a slower one. Yet it certainly does not follow—or at least I can't see how—that there is no motion at all."

Zeno responded to this objection with his "dichotomy" paradox.

Empirical evidence for overtaking tortoises

The dichotomy paradox

"Let's assume," says Zeno, "that Achilles—or anything else (it doesn't matter if it's a person, an airplane, or an arrow)—is supposed to pass through a certain distance, say from point A to point B." (See the diagram.) "In order to go from A to B Achilles must first pass through half the distance; that is, he must pass point C.

"But in order to pass a certain point, one must first reach it. That is, first he must go from A to C.

"But, in order to go from A to C, he must first pass through half the distance between them; that is, he must reach point D.

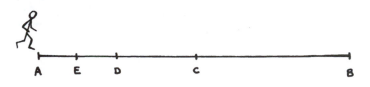

Achilles in the unstartable run

"And so on and so forth," says Zeno. "In order to pass through any distance, however minute, one must first pass through half of that distance. Yet to pass through the half, one must first pass through half of that half, and even before that, half of the half of the first half. And since 'moving' means going from one point to another, it follows that Achilles must pass through an infinite number of such halves in order to start moving.

"In other words, Achilles will never be able to start moving, since in order to move through even the first tiniest distance, he must pass through an infinite number of halves between himself and his goal (since any distance is divisible by two).

"Thus it turns out," Zeno concludes, "that even if we assume the existence of motion, we discover in the end that it is impossible, since no object can even begin to move. Therefore Parmenides is right—not only thanks to his own attack on the existence of motion, but because any other possible thesis will be faced with an insoluble paradox."

3
Descartes:
The Search for Certainty

Descartes was a seventeenth-century French philosopher who is generally considered the father of modern philosophy—the philosophy that reigned from the seventeenth century until the end of the nineteenth century. The distinguishing characteristic of this philosophy is that it is principally concerned with epistemology. In other words, instead of dealing directly with the essence of the world, modern philosophy begins by asking: "What method should we adopt for finding out about the world?" Descartes ascribed crucial importance to the method—more precisely, to the choice of the right method—by which it is possible to find out about the world.

In order to say something meaningful about the world, thought Descartes, I must begin my reasoning from some point of origin that I can rely on when discussing the nature of the world. But what is that point of origin, that first axiom, that I can use as a cornerstone of the cathedral of science and knowledge?

This point of origin must obviously be extremely solid and stable, as it constitutes the foundation of all reasoning and research. Therefore we must seek, thought Descartes, some certainty, some truth that absolutely cannot be doubted—and make this the springboard for the rest of our knowledge.

The limited framework of this introduction does not permit a thorough presentation of Descartes's method of building and consolidating his entire theory. Let us therefore concentrate on following his search for the "first philosophical truth" that is supposed to serve as the foundation for the entire program.

In order to make vivid the role of the first absolute truth, Descartes compared it, in his "Mediations," to the famous Archimedean point: "Archimedes demanded only one fixed and immobile point in order to move the earth from its place and transport it elsewhere. I too will be able to have high hopes if I succeed in discovering even one thing that is certain and indubitable.''

Well and good. If this is so, then the ''absolutely certain knowledge'' we are looking for is knowledge that cannot be doubted.

But how can we find such knowledge? And when we discover some piece of knowledge that seems certain to us, how can we make sure that no one will ever succeed in casting doubt upon it?

It seems, then, that we must initiate two processes: First, we must find some knowledge that seems to be an absolutely certain truth. Second, we must prove that no one will ever be able to cast any doubt upon it.

It's time now to go out and search for this certainty. So let's follow Descartes's ''Meditations'' on its journey in search of truth.

WE: So, Descartes, first we must ask how you intend to search for an absolutely certain truth. After all, many great philosophers have already dealt with this topic, and it has always happened that what appeared absolutely certain to one philosopher was considered quite doubtful, or even obviously false, by others. And since philosophers have been searching for certainty for over two thousand years, what makes you think that precisely we, with your guidance, will be privileged to attain such an absolute truth?

DESCARTES: The method.

WE: The method?

DESCARTES: Yes, the unique method by which we will search for this truth. Let me explain its uniqueness by a parable: Imagine a couple of miners standing near a great heap of sand, stones, and other materials all mixed together. These miners believe that somewhere in this great heap there is a precious diamond, and they are very eager to find it. Yet they know that many people have already searched through the heap from every possible direction—and still the desired diamond has not been found. Wouldn't they conclude from this that the diamond is probably covered with dust and so looks like an ordinary stone, so that it is difficult to distinguish from the other stones? Or that the diamond might be disguised some other way?

WE: That's very likely.

DESCARTES: It seems, then, think our miners, that we must search for the diamond in a different way from everyone else. Now listen to the method they propose: They will search for the diamond by using its unique quality—the fact that diamonds are the hardest substances known to man.

WE: This is quite puzzling; how can the miners make use of the diamond's unique hardness before they have even found it, since it isn't yet available for testing?

DESCARTES: The miners decide to build an iron stone-crusher and to pass the entire heap through this grinder. At the bottom of the grinder they fix a narrow grating through which all the sand and dust can pass. They reason that whatever material is crushed by the grinder and falls out cannot be the diamond. At the end, if any stone is left in the machine—a stone that is not ground up by its sharp blades but remains whole—they will know that the diamond they are seeking is in their hands!

Truth as a diamond

WE: You have shown us some very intelligent miners . . .

DESCARTES: Like ourselves, my dear friends. The miners in the fable are you and I, and the diamond they seek is the certainty we are looking for, whereas the rest of our beliefs are the pile of stones and gravel. We must now test them all, to see if there is any truth among them that is absolutely certain. This truth must be like the diamond: Just as the diamond is the hardest of all materials, and no other material can grind it up, so the outstanding characteristic of the absolutely certain truth is its stability; there is no argument strong enough to cast doubt upon it.

WE: And the grinder?

DESCARTES: We actually possess four grinders—four skeptical arguments to test the pile of our knowledge. Those pieces of knowledge that are undermined by any of our belief-crushers will be immediately cast aside; we have no need for them. This way we will finally be left with the desired certainty alone.

WE: Yet doesn't it seem ridiculous to use the tool of skepticism to attain the truth? Aren't there skeptical philosophers who claim that there is no such thing as "truth," and certainly not "absolutely certain truth"?

DESCARTES: We won't seem ridiculous if we find such a truth. But now let's get to work; let's put all our knowledge to the test of skepticism.

WE: But how can we test all our knowledge? Don't we know uncountably many things?

DESCARTES: Obviously we aren't going to test them one by one—we'll examine them in large groups. We'll start by testing the group of beliefs we've acquired through our senses—everything we've always considered most true and certain are things we've learned with the aid of our senses. Nevertheless, we sometimes discover that our senses are deceptive; for example, a stick placed in water seems bent in the middle, even though it is really just as straight as before.

WE: There's no shortage of such illusions.

DESCARTES: Then it won't seem implausible to assert that caution demands that we should never put our trust in anything by which we have once been deceived. And since the senses, as you have just admitted, do sometimes deceive us, we must disqualify them as unfit to give evidence. Thus all the knowledge we've gained through our sight, touch, hearing, smell, and taste—everything we know about the features of things—must be placed outside the bounds of our search. Does this seem reasonable to you?

WE: So far, at least, it seems quite reasonable.

DESCARTES: Then answer this: Aren't the empirical sciences based, at least partially, on what we grasp through our senses?

WE: Certainly.

DESCARTES: And haven't we just agreed that the senses are unfit to give evidence?

WE: Yes, we've agreed.

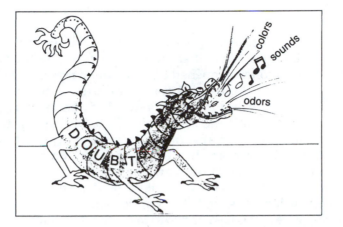

The dragon of doubt swallows up perceptual features

DESCARTES: Then it won't be wrong to conclude that physics, astronomy, medicine, and all the other sciences that are dependent on observation are dubious and uncertain, and that these sciences and all the knowledge we have gained from them must be disqualified for our use.

WE: Perhaps we can't rely on the empirical sciences; but it seems that we have already found an absolute certainty!

DESCARTES: And what is that?

WE: Let's say that this table we are now sitting around seems brown to us, but actually our eyes are deceiving us and it's really green. Let's also say that it seems warm to us, but actually it's cold.

DESCARTES: And so?

WE: But if we are really seeing and touching something, then even if we are mistaken about all its features, it is nevertheless certain that this thing exists! For instance, this table—even if some of its features are different from those reported by our senses, it's clear that at least the table itself exists. It seems, then, that this knowledge—that the table exists, even if its features are different from our perceptions—is the certainty we've been searching for.

DESCARTES: Here I'll have to use my argument from dreams, and remind you that we are human, and so we are in the habit of dreaming . . .

WE: And what of it?

DESCARTES: I must remember—and so must we all—that in my dreams I imagine things that are very far from the truth. For example, it has often happened that I've found myself right here in this room, fully dressed and seated by the fire, when in reality I was lying stark naked in bed! It's true that right now it seems quite clear to me that the eyes with which I'm looking at you are not filmy with sleep; that this head, which I'm now shaking, is not sunken in sleep; and that this hand, which I'm now raising with conscious intent, is really moving. . . .

But let each of us think now, with careful attention, if he has not seen such visions while he was sleeping.

To me, at least, this has happened many times, and when I think it over seriously, I can see that there are no definite signs by which to distinguish clearly between the states of wakefulness and sleep.

WE: And what follows from this?

DESCARTES: It follows that we can never determine with certainty whether we are awake or asleep.

WE: And the table?

DESCARTES: It also follows that even the existence of the table is not absolutely certain. Because if I am dreaming that I am touching and seeing it, then perhaps it doesn't exist at all. And since we cannot rule out the possibility that all of life is one long, extended dream, this is reason enough to cast doubt not only on the features of all things, but also on their very existence.

It's even possible that the various parts of my body—my eyes, my hands, my head—are nothing but products of my imagination; and so I can't even be sure that I have a body!

WE: Okay, let's set aside all corporeal objects and bodies, and everything else we've learned through the empirical sciences, and agree that it's right to cast doubt upon them. Even if that is the case, we may still be able to find certainty in the formal sciences. After all, arithmetic and geometry have almost always been considered true and reliable by almost all philosophers. For whether we are awake or dreaming, adding two and three will always yield five, and a square will never have more than four sides . . . It does not seem possible that such clear and apparent truth can be suspected of any falsity.

Doubt swallows up material objects as well

DESCARTES: This is a strong argument. The formal sciences really seem certain, and so does the knowledge that follows from them.

WE: You say "seem certain"? Do you doubt even them?

DESCARTES: Look at it this way: When we do slightly complicated arithmetical operations, say dividing 1579 by 142, doesn't it sometimes happen that we make mistakes?

WE: It happens.

DESCARTES: But according to the very same principle, we might be in error when we divide small numbers, such as 4 divided by 2, and other such simple operations. After all, there is no essential difference between the operation 1579 ÷ 142 and the operation 4 ÷ 2. I agree, of course, that the likelihood of error in 4 ÷ 2 is incomparably smaller than in complicated operations, but we still can't be totally certain that we do not sometimes make mistakes even with such simple operations.

WE: This time we can't accept your reasoning.

DESCARTES: And why not?

WE: In our humble opinion, if a particular individual has learned geometry and arithmetic, it is impossible for him to make any more mistakes in his calculations, especially not in such simple calculations as dividing 4 by 2. This seems absolutely certain to us! Of course, even the most gifted mathematician might make a mistake if someone deliberately prevented him from concentrating, or if someone hypnotized him without his awareness or influenced him psychologically in some other way.

DESCARTES: So be it—I accept this gladly! After all, hypnosis and psychological deception are also possibilities . . .

WE: Possibilities?

DESCARTES: Possibilities for justifying doubt! After all, I can't absolutely refute the possibility that there exists some evil demon—some creature who is no less powerful than deceitful, and who uses all his tricks to deceive me. And what if this demon has unlimited ability?—a possibility that can't be totally denied. How can I be sure that he isn't causing me, say by extended hypnosis, to make a mistake whenever I divide 4 by 2, or count the sides of a square, or make some even simpler judgment? After all, even this unlikely possibility is enough to prevent me from accepting the formal sciences and their propositions as absolutely indubitable certainties.

WE: Now you've really gone too far! This is really a much stranger hypothesis than anything we expected to hear.

DESCARTES: Yet we agreed from the outset not to accept anything that is not absolutely certain. And even this strange doubt is still a doubt—which is enough to disqualify all the formal sciences.

WE: But that's obvious! It's obvious that if we hypothesize a demon of this sort—or, even simpler, if we hypothesize that there's a God, and for reasons of His own He decides to cause us to err in all our judgments—then this possibility alone is sufficient to cast doubt not only on the truth of geometry and arithmetic but also on all our knowledge from whatever source and of whatever sort.

DESCARTES: And that's why it would be a good idea for all of us to suppose for a moment, in all seriousness, that the sky, the earth, colors, shapes, sounds, and all other external things are nothing but mirage and trickery, that a demon is using them to trick my innocent heart. The same is true of my own body—my eyes, my skin, my hands; I must believe that I have no organs or senses, that my belief in all these things is in error.

Mathematics is also infected . . .

WE: If so, then how can we continue to hope for any certainty whatsoever? After all, according to this system one can't even be certain of the existence of the demon—as this idea too is only a speculation. Obviously, if you continue to say, "Perhaps it is all a dream" and "Perhaps a demon is distorting all our perceptions" and other such weird "perhapses" as they occur to you—then every bit of our knowledge will be threatened.

Indubitably, Descartes, you can always cast doubt by this method, and so the chances of finding absolute certainty seem very low.

DESCARTES: Since you have affirmed this, there isn't much to add.

WE: What do you mean? Are you admitting that our search has failed?

DESCARTES: Failed? But you have already given us the answer!

WE: What answer? Let us remind you that the assertion we've finally arrived at was that by casting doubt we will never find absolute certainty . . .

DESCARTES: That's not what I meant. Actually, the answer is hidden in your previous assertion. Shall I repeat your words? You said, and I quote, "Indubitably, Descartes, you can always cast doubt by this method"—and the answer is hidden precisely here! For since you have asserted that there is one "indubitable" thing, we are now in possession of one thing, one piece of knowledge, that cannot be doubted!

WE: And that is the fact that we can always cast doubt?

DESCARTES: More or less. I think it would be best to express it this way: I cannot doubt the fact *that I am doubting*!

For if I try to doubt the fact that I am doubting, then this very attempt demonstrates the existence of doubting! In other words, my attempt to doubt the existence of doubting only serves to demonstrate that an act of doubting exists.

Will it eliminate itself?

WE: Great! Then we've found an absolute certainty! And we admit that it certainly seems like one. But now we come to the second part of the proof: You must show that no one can argue the contrary—seriously contend that this piece of knowledge is also open to challenge.

DESCARTES: Nothing is easier than that! For if anyone claims that this piece of knowledge—the fact that an act of doubting exists—might be wrong, won't he be expressing his doubt of this fact?

WE: Yes.

DESCARTES: And when he says this, isn't he claiming that he's doubting the possibility of doubting?

WE: And that is absolutely incoherent! Good God! No one can challenge this truth, for the very act of doubting it affirms it!

DESCARTES: And if you think for a moment, you can find some other truths whose certainty can be proven with the same reasoning.

WE: Absolutely! By the same reasoning we also cannot doubt the fact that we are thinking! Or that there are thoughts in the world. For doubting these propositions is equivalent to saying: "We think that we aren't thinking," which is self-contradictory. We can therefore state with absolute certainty: We think!

DESCARTES: Excellent. And now we can also assert that even if our hypothesis of the vicious demon is true and this powerful demon is constantly using every possible trick to deceive me, there is no doubt that I exist, if he is deceiving me. No matter how much he deceives me, he can never turn me into nothing as long as I think that I am something. Therefore, after we've delved into the heart of the matter, and after we've examined everything carefully, we must finally decide that these propositions—*"I exist"* and *"I am a thinking and doubting being"*—are necessarily true every time I pronounce or conceive them. This, ladies and gentlemen, is our Archimedean point, the first ultimate truth, which will serve as a foundation for our search for knowledge.

*

The end of doubt: the above dialogue presented the process of casting doubt and the eventual discovery of "the first philosophical truth." The course of the dialogue is based in large measure on Descartes's own arguments in the first two chapters of his "Meditations."

You must be very curious to know what is in the remaining four chapters of this little book. How did Descartes use the "Archimedean point" as a foundation for knowledge—"to establish something firm and permanent in the sciences," as he put it? The best way for you to satisfy your curiosity would be simply to read the "Mediations," but in order not to leave you in suspense we'll present a short summary of its basic ideas.

The problem confronting Descartes after finding his Archimedean point was the fact that this knowledge referred only to himself. Everything he knew for certain began with "I"—"I exist," "I think," "I want," "I feel," and so on. How could he extend his knowledge from the internal "I" to the external world? Could he know something about it as well? How could he even confirm its very existence?

Descartes's solution is original and quite odd; he goes from the Archimedean point to the external world through God.

"God?" you may ask. "What role could God play in this drama? And besides, how does our skeptic Descartes know that God exists?" Well, in the third chapter of the "Meditations" Descartes proves the existence of God. He does not even rest content with one proof of it, but presents three different arguments for God's existence! Here's one of them:

Descartes says to himself: "I have a notion of 'God' in my mind whose meaning is something infinite, omnipotent, omniscient, and so on. Where can this notion come from? Can I myself be its source? Is it possible that I invented it in my imagination? Or could I have dreamt it, the way I might be dreaming the existence of all the world around me?"

Descartes's answer is in the negative. He knows that he himself is neither infinite nor omnipotent, because if he were he would have known everything from the outset, with no doubts whatsoever. "Since I myself am a finite being," says Descartes to himself, "it is beyond my capacity to invent the idea of infinity by myself. Why? Because only an infinite entity is capable of encompassing infinity in its mind and of creating, accordingly, a notion of it. Hence only God Himself can be the creator of the idea of infinity, and it is therefore He who put this concept into my mind. That is, since I have a notion of an infinite God, and since only God could have been the generator of this notion, it follows that God exists!"

Is this convincing?

If not, it is certainly at least an intriguing method of proof. From this point Descartes proceeds to another judgment about God: "God is not deceitful." And why not? Because, according to Descartes, "Deceitfulness is necessarily connected with some sort of fault," while God, who is infinite by definition, is perfect and faultless.

Thus it seems that God exists and that He can't be deceitful; but what about the external world—does it exist or not?

If God is not deceitful, Descartes answers himself, then He surely did not create the world in a way that would lead us into profound and extensive errors. But there is no doubt that most people are absolutely convinced of the existence of things outside themselves; that is, of material objects. Our senses are also structured in such a way that they are constantly hinting at the existence of a world outside the "I" which contains matter and objects. "I don't see," says Descartes, "how one could absolve God of deceitfulness if these concepts (such as most sensory perceptions) were actually generated not by material objects but rather by other causes. Therefore it is evident that the external world exists, since the good God is not deceitful."

Thus Descartes's doubts have come to an end. Descartes can sleep peacefully—he exists, the world exists, and a benevolent omnipotent God watches over them. But what about those of us who do not accept Descartes's proofs of the existence of God? Or of God's trustworthiness? All these people—and this includes most philosophers after Descartes—are left with their doubts, in the stage at which we ended our dialogue:

I exist, I think, I sense.

But is there anything else?

Are there other people out there?

Are there bodies and objects here?

All these are questions that Descartes has left us with, and it seems that no one has yet found a conclusive reply to them.

4

Hume: Cause?

David Hume, a Scottish philosopher who lived after Descartes and Berkeley, is considered a member of the Empiricist trend, together with Locke, Berkeley, and Mill. The Empiricists claim that we learn about the world through our senses. They see the main role of philosophy as studying the learning process through which we find out about the structure, features, and laws of our world through our sense impressions.

These philosophers, however, did not denigrate the "formal sciences," such as mathematics and logic. Hume in fact even claimed that mathematics is necessarily true and certain because it deals with numbers, which are ideas in our minds. But studying mathematics does not contribute to our knowledge about factual reality, since that science deals only with abstract numbers and not with real objects.

The main question that bothered Hume was this: How do we learn about the real world, about the world of events, objects, and features?

It seems to me that it would be best if we invited Hume to have a discussion with a scientist whose job it is to find out about nature, and wrote down their discussion in their own words:

HUME: So, Mr. Scientist, how can we find out about the world?

SCIENTIST: Obviously, in order to get to know about the world, we have to look at it carefully; and how do we look? We look at the physical world, at the world of facts and events, with our bodily senses—the five senses that tell us about our surroundings.

HUME: Your answer leads straight to my main problem, since this is exactly what is hard for me to understand: How can our senses teach us anything worthwhile?

SCIENTIST: This sounds like a dialogue between two halfwits. I can't understand how you can possibly fail to understand such a simple matter.

HUME: I'll try to explain. You say that we can grasp and know the world through our senses . . .

SCIENTIST: Right.

HUME: But if we accept the claim of our colleague George Berkeley, we'll agree that all we can grasp through our senses are our impressions—and that we can never know what is behind them.

SCIENTIST: That's also true.

HUME: Shall we agree, then, that the only thing our senses can give us is our impressions? Our sense impressions and nothing else? That is, where sight is concerned, all we have is pictures; and where hearing is concerned, all we have is sounds; and that the same holds true for all the other senses?

SCIENTIST: That's clear.

HUME: Then we are left with two options: We can argue against Berkeley and claim that there is a real material world behind our sense impressions. But then we will have to admit that we can't get to know this world through our senses, contrary to your suggestion at the beginning of our talk. The other option is to agree with Berkeley at least to some extent, and to declare that the world that interests us is just the totality of our impressions— that is, what we grasp, or what can be grasped, through our senses.

SCIENTIST: Well, it may surprise you, but I gladly agree with Berkeley. I see no point in assuming the existence of "objects" beyond the scope of science. And science, as I said at the beginning, consists entirely of learning through observation and experiment.

HUME: So you agree with Berkeley . . .

SCIENTIST: Only on this one issue: that there is no point in assuming the existence of things which can't be grasped or perceived. But what's wrong with that? If we agree to that, then it turns out that everything in the world can be encountered and grasped. To be honest, I find the philosophical debate about objective reality quite futile. The debate about the existence of material objects beyond our impressions, things which resemble them, or the nonexistence of such things, should not affect our picture of the world anyway.

HUME: I don't agree with that.

SCIENTIST: With what?

HUME: I don't think you can find out everything you want and expect just through your sense impressions.

SCIENTIST: Aha, I see you missed something. You forgot that I declared in advance that the only things of interest to science are the things that can be grasped—that is, sense impressions. This implies that we can find out about them through our senses, as we have agreed that our senses grasp impressions.

HUME: Yet I am convinced that whether we assume that the world is made up entirely of impressions, or whether it also contains matter—in either case there is something that we can't find out about through our senses.

SCIENTIST: And what's that?

HUME: Something of supreme importance—what scientists look for more than anything else.

SCIENTIST: And what is it that I'm looking for more than anything else?

HUME: Causes.

SCIENTIST: Causes of what? What causes are you talking about?

HUME: All of them! I claim that it's impossible to find out about causes through the senses.

SCIENTIST: That sounds really strange. I hope you have a good explanation ready . . .

HUME: I'll tell you my reason in a minute. But first let's clarify what we mean by the word "cause." When we say that a certain event A is the cause of event B, we mean that A brought about B, or that it was responsible in one way or another for the generation of B. Does this seem right to you?

SCIENTIST: Yes, but that is hardly a definition. All you said was that "brought about" and "generated" are synonyms of "caused."

HUME: All right, perhaps it would be better if we defined "cause" negatively, and said this: If event A is the cause of event B, this means that if A had not occurred and in other respects the world had been exactly the same, then B would not have occurred either.

SCIENTIST: Bravo! That's a good definition. This is certainly the meaning of the word "cause."

HUME: Then does our agreement imply that causation is a kind of relation? A relation between two events?

SCIENTIST: Absolutely.

HUME: The time has come, then, to give a specific example of this relation. I am now going to bang my fist on this wooden table—see? (Here Hume raises his fist and bangs on the table, making a loud noise.)

The movement is seen

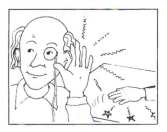
The blow is heard

SCIENTIST: You bet!

HUME: And you heard the noise too?

SCIENTIST: Well, I'm not deaf.

HUME: And don't people usually say in such a case that the blow on the table was the cause of the noise? That my hitting the table brought about the noise?

SCIENTIST: And they're absolutely right. In this case there isn't any doubt that it was your hitting the table that caused the noise.

HUME: "There isn't any doubt?" How can you be so sure?

SCIENTIST: What else could have been the cause?

HUME: Look, we've agreed that we find out about the world through our senses. We've also agreed that all that our senses can provide us are impressions, and nothing else. Now here, in this particular case, our senses have provided us with two distinct impressions: the first, the sight of my hand hitting the table; and the second, a loud noise received by our ears.

SCIENTIST: That's a faithful account of what happened. But what does it imply?

HUME: Did we have another impression besides the two mentioned above?

SCIENTIST: No.

HUME: Then all we have are two impressions or sensations.

SCIENTIST: And what's wrong with that?

HUME: Look, we had one impression of a hand approaching and touching the table, and another impression of a noise. But we didn't have any impression of a causal link between the two. We did not sense with any of our senses the supposed relation of causality between the hitting of the table and the loud noise. Therefore we have no way of knowing that the blow was the actual cause of the noise.

SCIENTIST: But it's very reasonable; it's most likely that it was the hitting of the table that caused the noise.

HUME: Most likely? What makes you think so? All we have before us are our impressions, which consist of colors, shadows, sounds, voices, and so on. But I don't see any causality or likelihood among them.

SCIENTIST: Well, it might be wrong to infer causality between two distinct events on the basis of just one instance. Apparently we derive it from many repeated experiments.

HUME: But even repeated experiments only contain impressions—including colors, sounds, and the like—but not causality.

SCIENTIST: No, this time I can't accept your judgment. Besides these impressions, our experience also contains some cumulative learning from the past. For example, since I have seen countless times that hitting a wooden table very hard is accompanied by noise, this very repetition of the phenomenon—that the noise comes after the blow—teaches me that the blow is the cause of the noise. Surely you wouldn't say it's possible for two types of event to occur one after the other so many times without there being any link between them. Such a claim would be absurd.

HUME: With all due respect, my dear sir, this is precisely what I'm claiming—that it is plausible!

SCIENTIST: I think I am beginning to understand why some people say that doing philosophy is wrestling with the absurd. For could any sane person believe that in all the hundreds of times he has heard a loud noise after someone banged on a table, it has always occurred by chance? Could it be just a coincidence that these two events appeared together thousands of times?

HUME: Well, why not?

SCIENTIST: Here's another good reason: Not only do we always see the hand hitting the table and hear the noise at almost exactly the same time, but there is a fixed order to these events. Every time this occurs, the hitting of the table, or our impression of it, precedes our impression of the noise. Thus, it's absolutely impossible for chance to be involved in such an orderly recurrence, which seems to remain constant so many times!

HUME: And why not?

SCIENTIST: Really, this is becoming ridiculous. But okay—let me show you why not. You claim that chance is at the bottom of all this, don't you?

HUME: Not exactly. What I do claim is that perhaps it occurred by chance, and that at any rate it will be difficult for you to prove the contrary.

SCIENTIST: Not necessarily. Look—let's assume for the moment that it was due to chance. If so, then you have no reason to predict another noise when I hit the table again in a minute. Are you actually committing yourself to the claim that you don't know whether a noise will be heard when I hit the table in a minute?

HUME: That's right—I don't predict it.

SCIENTIST: But I, on the other hand, do commit myself to the opposite claim. Since I assume that the blow is the cause of the noise, I must predict that when I hit the table the noise will follow again.

HUME: I accept that these must be our stands.

SCIENTIST: Then let's allow an objective scientific experiment to decide whose assumption is more nearly correct: mine, which predicts with complete certainty that every time I hit the table a noise will ensue; or yours, which claims that chance may be involved; and just as it is possible that there will be a noise, it is also possible that in some of the cases there won't be.

HUME: If you want to perform an experiment, who am I to object? Go ahead . . .

Hume   The scientist

At this point the scientist went over to the solid wooden table and hit it with his fist, and a loud noise was immediately heard. The scientist picked up his hand and hit the table again, and again a noise ensued; and he did it again and again until his hand became red and sore. Then he spoke again.

SCIENTIST: Do you see? The noise was not absent even once. Just as I predicted, it appeared immediately after the blow.

HUME: And what can you deduce from that?

SCIENTIST: If chance had been involved previously, then it would have been reasonable to assume that in at least some of the present cases there wouldn't have been any noise. But since this did not happen even once, it may be concluded that the blow to the table brings about the noise; that is, that the blow is the actual cause of the noise.

HUME: It seems to me that your joy is premature. Couldn't chance have been involved again?

SCIENTIST: No! I'm absolutely sure that if I hit the table once more, we'll hear the noise again. Look! Look and listen! (The scientist hits the table once again, and the familiar noise is heard . . .)

HUME: Well, couldn't it have been a coincidence this time too?

SCIENTIST: Are you making fun of me? Will you continue to argue, every time I repeat the experiment, that it *might* have been due to chance? It seems to me that you'll have to offer better reasons for this claim.

Obviously you can always jump up and say: "Due to chance . . . a matter of chance. . . ." But don't you admit that no assertion has any value unless it is supported by a good argument?

HUME: I agree willingly.

SCIENTIST: Great! Then what is the argument for your assertion?

HUME: Which assertion?

SCIENTIST: The one we're talking about! That in every case when we heard the noise right after we saw the hand hitting the table, it was only a coincidence that the two phenomena occurred together—your assertion that there is no causal link between the blow and the following noise.

HUME: You are accusing me unjustly! I never made such an assertion.

SCIENTIST: Wonder of wonders! And what then did you assert a moment ago?

HUME: I asserted only one thing—that I am not able to make any assertions. That's why I kept saying that *perhaps* the coupling of these phenomena came about by chance, and perhaps not. And why can't I come to a decisive stand about this? Precisely because I don't have any solid reason at my disposal to explain why the two phenomena occurred in that particular order so many times.

But you have actually risked making decisive assertions—since you have asserted explicitly that the blow is the cause of the noise that follows it. Therefore, in accordance with your comment— that we should have good arguments for our assertions—I must ask you: What is your argument for your assertion?

The scientist appears somewhat baffled, and there is silence for a while, until Hume speaks again.

HUME: My dear friend, let's spare ourselves any additional table banging, as these recurrent experiments are like banging our heads against the wall. For my part, I'm willing to assume that we've hit the poor table countless times, and that the noise has always followed the blow. Nevertheless, I still hold fast to my demand that you provide a good argument for your assertion that chance played no part, or at least not the crucial part, in most of these cases.

SCIENTIST: And can you tell me how to justify something that is so simple and obvious—except to those few people who do philosophy?

HUME: I'm sorry to disappoint you, but I don't see any justification on the horizon.

SCIENTIST: Please answer me honestly: Do you really believe it was just a coincidence that every time we hit the table we heard the noise afterwards? After all, even a skeptical philosopher like you must admit that in your daily life you don't really act as though you believe in absolute chance!

HUME: Must there be a connection between my everyday beliefs and behavior and our argument? We're not talking about beliefs but about ideas and knowledge, so let's concern ourselves only with my reasons.

SCIENTIST: I admit that I am quite perplexed, but I will still risk saying that it seems totally implausible that something should occur in a particular order over and over again without a specific cause. Your hypothesis just doesn't make sense. First—and this is clear and agreed upon by everyone—everything that exists must have a cause. For what could have brought any given thing into being if there was no cause for it?

  Listen carefully: I'm not presuming that scientists will discover the specific cause of each and every event; I'm not even claiming that it's within our power to find out all the causes in the universe. I'm just speaking about a matter of principle: that it's absolutely inconceivable that anything will occur or come into being without some prior thing or state of affairs which created it and brought it about. This necessity is beyond any doubt!

Therefore we can conclude that this is also the case with the phenomenon at hand, as well as with every phenomenon.

But here Hume interrupted: "Beyond any doubt"—sharp words. You assert: "Everything must have a cause." Yet a while ago you claimed that every assertion needs a proof. Can you prove this last assertion of yours?

SCIENTIST: Of course. Just let me think a minute . . .

HUME: Let me help a little. Do you agree that your proposition "Everything must have a cause" is equivalent to "There can be nothing in the world without a cause?"

SCIENTIST: Obviously they're equivalent.

HUME: Then in order to prove that "everything has a cause," what you actually need to prove is that "there can be nothing without a cause."

SCIENTIST: And I take it upon myself to prove this.

HUME: And I claim that it is impossible to prove it.

SCIENTIST: Finally you too have made an assertion! Now I can rest for a while and transfer the burden of proof from my shoulders to yours. I demand that you prove this assertion of yours: that it's impossible to prove that "everything has a cause!"

HUME: Well, perhaps I spoke too hastily. I'm not able to prove conclusively that it's impossible to prove that "everything has a cause." Let me say only this: that I don't see how it's possible to prove it. You must understand that in order to test this proposition experimentally you would have to examine all the objects and events in the entire universe and find a cause for each one. This seems to be an impossible task, since there is an infinite number of objects and events.

SCIENTIST: I accept the argument. The proof I intend is not an empirical one but rather a rational and principled proof. I think I have a philosophical argument demonstrating the impossibility of anything without a cause.

HUME: I'm very curious to hear it.

SCIENTIST: Tell me, then, do you agree that if we claim that there is something without a cause, then we are actually claiming that no previous thing brought it about or created it?

HUME: I agree.

SCIENTIST: And thus we would be claiming that this thing created itself, since there is no other thing that created it. Thus what we are really saying about it is that it is the cause of itself! And this is an explicit contradiction—that something should be the cause of itself.

HUME: I see what you are saying. Your argument has two stages:
A) If there is something without a cause, then it's the cause of itself.
B) It's impossible for something to be the cause of itself.
Thus you conclude: There is nothing without a cause.

SCIENTIST: That's precisely what I said; is it possible not to accept it?

HUME: It doesn't seem right to me.

SCIENTIST: And what precisely doesn't seem right?

HUME: Stage A. Why do you say that "if there is something without a cause, then it's the cause of itself?"

SCIENTIST: Because if we assume that it does not have an external cause, then the only option left is that it is the cause of itself.

HUME: There's a third option.

SCIENTIST: Namely?

HUME: That it is not the cause of itself, but rather that it has no cause at all.

SCIENTIST: That's completely impossible—everything has to have some cause!—Oh, wait a minute. . . . I'm sorry; that proposition is what I wanted to prove.

HUME: That's precisely the proposition you were trying to prove—that "everything has some cause." You can't support your proof by the very thing you are trying to prove!

SCIENTIST: All right, I've already seen the fly in the ointment. But I think I have another argument, and I believe it's better than the one we disqualified. Are you still willing to listen?

HUME: Certainly!

SCIENTIST: This time let's assume that there is something without a cause, and that it is not even the cause of itself—that it is, as you suggested, something entirely without a cause.

HUME: Very well.

SCIENTIST: Now, do you remember Parmenides' dilemma: "Everything must be created either from something or from nothing"?

HUME: I remember it well.

SCIENTIST: When we claim that there is something without a cause, then we are claiming, aren't we, that nothing created that thing? That is, that it wasn't created by any being?

HUME: That's our claim.

SCIENTIST: Then, according to Parmenides' dilemma, there is no escape from saying that this thing was created from nothing?

HUME: Certainly, according to Parmenides.

SCIENTIST: But surely you accept Parmenides' claim that "the nothing does not exist"?

HUME: Yes.

SCIENTIST: Then it's impossible that something was created from nothing.

HUME: I accept that.

SCIENTIST: Let's summarize our position: We have seen that when we say that something has no cause, this implies that the thing was created out of nothing. But this is impossible, because the nothing does not exist. From this we can deduce that it is totally absurd to say that there could be something without a cause.

HUME: Okay. And all this is based on Parmenides' dilemma that "everything is created either from something or from nothing"?

SCIENTIST: And don't you accept Parmenides? Is there a third option?

HUME: Yes, definitely—that there is something that wasn't created at all, either from something or from nothing.

SCIENTIST: But that is totally absurd! This fantastic assertion contradicts the law of conservation of mass! Everything must have its origin somewhere, in something it was generated or created from.

HUME: Are you able to prove that?

SCIENTIST: I'll try.

HUME: But don't you see that the premise you and Parmenides share, that "everything was created from something," is equivalent to the assumption that "everything has a cause," a cause that created it? . . . Why don't you answer me?

The scientist was silent. Afterwards he nodded and said in despair: I see.

HUME: But this is exactly what you were trying to prove: that "everything has a cause." Once more, then, you assumed from the outset the very thing you were trying to prove.

SCIENTIST: If that is the case, then I'll have to give up. I can't prove it.

HUME: But if we can't be certain that "everything has a cause," then, as we saw before, without the assistance of this rule we won't be able to prove the existence of causality with certainty even in specific cases! We won't be able to show that one of any two specific events is the cause of the other—as we saw in the case of the hand hitting the table and the ensuing noise.

SCIENTIST: That's right.

HUME: . . . Since we will always have to consider the possibility that chance was involved, even if it happened many times.

SCIENTIST: I can't argue with you.

HUME: Then do you agree that we will never be able to find out whether a certain thing is the cause of another thing?

SCIENTIST: Okay, that is already implied by what we said before.

HUME: And therefore we must conclude that we will never discover even one single cause.

SCIENTIST: How absolutely awful! This implies that we will never know anything about nature and how it works. But I have to admit that there's nothing I can do about it. I simply give up. . . .

*

In reading this dialogue we've learned that Hume has good reasons for his claim that we will never be able to find out and understand the specific causes of things and events. But how is this related to the explicit aim of science: the discovery and formulation of the laws of nature? If Hume is right, then science is faced with considerable difficulties.

Let's reconstruct, with the aid of an example, the way scientists arrive at their discoveries and formulations of the laws of nature. Consider the law that "water boils at 100°C at atmospheric pressure." How is this law proved? The proof of every scientific law can be divided into three stages:

The hypothesis stage
The experimental testing stage
The inference stage

In the example we are using, the three stages look like this:

The hypothesis: Water boils at 100°C at atmospheric pressure.

The experimental test: We have seen that every time we inspected water at 100°C and atmospheric pressure, it boiled (that is, it began to bubble).

The inference: Whenever water is brought to 100°C at atmospheric pressure, it will boil.

The problem, according to Hume, is that the conclusion is much more far-reaching than the proof or the inspection, since the inspection refers to a thousand specific cases, whereas the conclusion refers both to these cases and to an infinite number of additional cases. In other words, the findings of our inspection are not sufficient to warrant the conclusion.

When scientists draw conclusions in this way, they necessarily rely on additional assumptions, assumptions that were mostly unconscious before Hume. The additional assumptions are these:

1. Everything must have a cause.
2. A specific cause A must always have the same effect B.

Using these assumptions, scientists can derive their conclusions as follows: They determine in advance that the boiling of water has a cause, according to Rule 1. After many trials in which they bring about the boiling of water at 100°C at atmospheric pressure, under various conditions and at various times, they reach the conclusion that bringing water to 100°C at atmospheric pressure is the cause, and a sufficient cause, of the event of its boiling.

Since the scientists also assume "once a cause, always a cause" for the same event (Rule 2), they draw the following final conclusion: "Water will always boil at 100°C at atmospheric pressure," and this conclusion is valid even for cases that have not been inspected.

But remember: This is true only under the condition that the two additional assumptions, Rules 1 and 2, are true—that is, on condition that "everything has a cause" and "once a cause, always a cause." However, these assumptions cannot be proved, as we saw in the dialogue, and so scientists may not rely on them—since it is possible that they are wrong.

Thus scientists are not able to prove even one scientific law, and they are not able to predict how nature will work, or how any machine will work, tomorrow or the next day.

5

Kant:
Knowing the World—
How Is It Possible?

One of philosophy's essential features is concern with theoretical and abstract problems, problems that nonphilosophers are apt to react to with a shrug of their shoulders, or at most with the question: "Why should I care about that?" Philosophers, on the other hand, are disturbed by the existence of these problems and struggle to solve them throughout their lives.

One of these abstract problems is "knowledge through experience": Can we know the world around us and its laws? Can we trust our empirical cognitions to lead us to the truth? These ancient questions were reinforced by Hume's assault on the concept of causality.

The German philosopher Immanuel Kant considered these problems with profound concern. His primary goal was to solve Hume's difficulties: to explain how experiential knowledge is possible and how we can be sure that such knowledge is true.

Kant was influenced by Hume in his philosophical thought, adopting Hume's views on numerous issues. He accepted, for instance, the Humean stand concerning the impossibility of deriving the concept of causality from experience. Likewise, Kant adopted Hume's view of the decisive importance of the concept of causality for scientific knowledge and learning from experience.

What led Kant to a different theory from Hume's was mainly his distinct point of origin. This is evident from the difference between Hume's and Kant's basic assumptions. While Hume asked the skeptical question, "Is knowledge of the world possible?" (and his answer was basically "No"), Kant shifted the question to "How is knowledge of the world possible?"

Thus Kant presupposed that there is experiential knowledge and that it is of some value. The task he took upon himself was entirely positive: to discover and describe the mechanism for acquiring experiential knowledge. He assumed that the very discovery of this mechanism might provide evidence for its validity as well. The stress is thus shifted from the skeptical Humean question of "whether" to the optimistic Kantian question of "how."

The answer to this question—in other words, Kant's theory of epistemology—is very complex, and so we will be able to present only its main principles in a very general way.

*

Hume's picture of science can be compared to an inverted pyramid, standing on its point. At its narrow base are the laws of nature, such as "Everything has a cause," which applies to all possible events. In the middle are laws that apply to parts of reality, such as the law stating that moving objects will continue to move uniformly as long as they are not disturbed by an external force. Near the wide top of the inverted pyramid are particular laws, such as "Water boils at 100°C," which applies only to water.

Why an inverted pyramid?

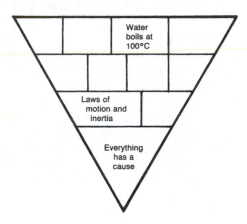

The hierarchy of the laws of nature

Because, as we saw in the previous chapter, the derivation of a scientific law relies not only on observational data, but also on the stipulations: "Everything has a cause" and "If A is once a cause of B, then A is always a cause of B." These stipulations form the point of support which serves as a basis for all of science. If they were wrong, the entire scientific pyramid would lose its base, topple over, and be shattered to splinters. Hume, as we have seen, does not see any way to guarantee their validity.

It seems, then, that this model puts scientists in a very frustrating position: They are able to derive the more particular laws—which are the least interesting—from empirical evidence, by presupposing the validity of the more general laws. However, the most general laws of the universe—the ones that are the most interesting—they are unable to prove!

Here Kant enters the picture:

KANT: Obviously, if science really is based on certain stipulations and is dependent on their validity, it follows that there is no hope for scientific confirmation of these stipulations. If every scientific proof presupposes that "everything has a cause," then any attempt at a scientific proof of it will be using this very assertion, and so will be guilty of circular reasoning.

WE: What do you mean?

KANT: Science cannot prove its own general validity. In order for a scientific proof of this to be valid, its validity must already have been proved before we set out to prove it, which leads to a vicious circle.

We must also amend Hume's scientific picture: At the basis of science there are several additional assumptions whose status is similar to that of Hume's two laws of causality, in that the very possibility and correctness of science is based on them, and therefore they cannot be scientifically proved.

WE: And what are they?

KANT: I don't have time to present all of them, but I'll mention two important areas of stipulation: geometry and arithmetic. I have no doubt that geometry and arithmetic are necessary conditions for the scientific endeavor, and therefore I claim that their axioms belong at the base of the scientific pyramid, alongside the laws of causality.

WE: Even if we agree that science is not capable of proving the validity of these axioms, it does not necessarily follow that the status of these rules is the same as that of the laws of causality.

KANT: And what is the difference between them?

WE: First, we aren't sure that geometry and arithmetic are necessary conditions of science. But more important, geometry and arithmetic seem to be true a priori—that is, not derived from observations. Rather, the truth of geometry and arithmetic follows from the fact that their axioms and basic concepts are innate. Their theorems are derived from their axioms and postulates, and this enables us to verify unambiguously the truth or falsity of every proposition written in their language.

In contrast, the assumptions "everything has a cause" and "if A is once a cause of B, then A is always a cause of B" do not seem to be a priori, and we already saw in the discussion with Hume how the scientist failed in his attempt to prove the rule that "everything has a cause" by using a rational, a priori method.

KANT: In my opinion, the two laws of causality are a priori in exactly the same way as arithmetic and geometry. But their status is not like that of geometric theorems; rather, it is like that of the axioms themselves. For on the one hand everyone uses these assumptions every day, when they assume their validity (generally without explicit awareness); and on the other hand we've already agreed with Hume that it's impossible to derive them from experience.

WE: But even if we accept this argument, we still say that there is no connection between arithmetic and geometry on the one hand, and science on the other. Science is not based on arithmetic and geometry, because the two apply to things that are totally different.

KANT: What do you mean?

WE: Science is entirely concerned with objects and events that exist and take place in the real, objective world. The laws discovered by science refer to mass and motion, to different materials and their compounds, to stars, to water, and so on.

Arithmetic and geometry, on the other hand, do not tell us anything about the material world, but deal with ideas that are the product of the human intellect and exist in our minds. Arithmetic and geometry are about such things as lines and points devoid of volume or area, or such things as numbers, sums, and roots. These concepts have no existence in the material world, apart from being ideas in our heads. Therefore arithmetic and geometry have nothing to do with science, since they do not contain any information about the subject of science, which is the universe.

KANT: But this is not true at all. The theorems of arithmetic and geometry definitely do contain information about the material world surrounding us. I even think that this information is vital for the conduct of science.

Here's a simple example showing how arithmetic can be used to find out a fact about the world. Let's say Sarah is picking apples and putting them into a closed basket. At first she picks seven apples and puts them into the basket. Then she sees another five apples, picks them, and places them in the basket. At this point someone asks her how many apples are in the basket.

Obviously there are two different ways to find out. The first is basically observational—she could lift up the cover of the basket and get a visual impression of the number of apples in it. The second is basically computational—she could perform a computation based on the observations of the past and on arithmetic. That is, she could rely on her memory of the occasions on which she put a certain number of apples into the basket, translate this memory into arithmetical language—that is, into the numbers 7 and 5—and use the arithmetical statement (which is essentially a priori) that 7 + 5 = 12. As a result of this calculation Sarah could conclude that she has a dozen apples in her basket, without going to the trouble of performing an additional observation. Thus we can conclude that Sarah has derived the outcome of a future observation by relying on the rules of arithmetic, and so arithmetic does contain information about the real world.

In the same way, using more complicated mathematics, scientists can obtain information and use it to construct predictions about the orbits of the planets, the speed of chemical reactions, and every other physical process of this type.

Do you understand now why arithmetic and geometry are so vital for science?

WE: But now we confront Hume's previous question even more forcefully: How do we know that the laws of causality are correct and that we are justified in using them to learn about the world?

The same question can be raised about geometry and arithmetic as well: How do we know that the information they provide us with is correct? Where do we get our certainty that their use always leads us to true assertions about the world?

KANT: We can claim that they are true if we succeed in showing that there is a general and necessary coordination between the a priori domain in our reason and the real world.

WE: But how can there be a coordination between two things as different as material existence on the one hand and the a priori laws of reason on the other? Aren't the latter the mere products of our thought?

KANT: There must be such a coordination, because otherwise neither science nor learning of any kind would be possible.

WE: Nevertheless, it's impossible to imagine how there can be any sort of fit between two realms that are so different and so distant from each other. After all, you yourself admit that the real world and our observations of it have no influence on the development of arithmetic and geometry, or the formation of the laws of causality!

KANT: I do believe that.

WE: Then it follows that the creation of such a fit is impossible, for the world cannot influence the a priori realm and affect our a priori laws, in order to fit them to reality.

KANT: So there is only one possibility left . . .

WE: What's that? What possibility?

KANT: When a high degree of coordination is discovered between two things, call them W and M, and when a search for the cause of this coordination reveals that there is no possibility that W could affect M, what can be deduced from this? [We chose W and M to stand for world and mind.]

WE: That such coordination is impossible.

KANT: But it exists and we can see it in front of our eyes! We must find an explanation for it.

WE: We don't see how.

KANT: I believe we are compelled to draw the following conclusion: Since the direction of fit is not in the influence of W on M, as such an influence is impossible, it must be in the opposite direction—that is, in the influence of M on W!

WE: Well, that is also a possibility. That is . . .

KANT: That is . . . when we have reached the conclusion that the world does not influence our a priori reason, we must infer that it is our pure reason that acts upon and influences the world.

WE: You're talking nonsense! How can our reason and its laws influence the world? In order to do that we would have to be able to compel the entire universe to act in accordance with the laws of our reason, which would mean that we would be gods!

With all due respect, Kant, we don't understand what you mean. How could you possibly imagine that our reason compels the sun and the planets, for example, to move according to its a priori laws?

KANT: I will gladly explain my position—if you'll just have a little patience. . . . In order to explain how this fit is generated, I will have to make use of a parable: Assume that someone, myself for example, is wandering around with glasses covered with green cellophane. How will the objects around me look?

WE: Greenish, of course.

KANT: Would I then be justified in basing my judgment on my experience and claiming that the world is as green as it looks to me?

WE: Only as a joke. For it's obvious to all of us that the illusion is created by the green glasses, and when you take them off the world will revert to its true colors once again.

KANT: Okay. Now let's go a step further: Assume that I'm unable to take off the glasses.

WE: What's stopping you from taking them off?

KANT: Let's assume that, just as some people are born color-blind, someone was born with green lenses in his eyes. Wouldn't it be plausible to assert that to this person everything in the world would be tinged with green?

WE: That's true, but just as in cases of color-blindness, this defect would eventually be discovered. The person's friends would let him know that there are many colors that he is unable to distinguish. In the end this unfortunate person would realize that the world is colored differently from the way he sees it.

KANT: You're forcing me to add another appendix to the story: Assume that all people, at all times, have been born with green lenses in their eyes. Would you still say that the world seems green to them although it is actually many-colored?

WE: This is a genuine puzzle. How could these people imagine that the true reality is not their subjective green-tinged reality? There wouldn't be anyone to tell them of their mistake.

KANT: In my opinion, in a case like this there is no longer any point in talking about two levels of reality. It makes no sense to distinguish between a theoretical true reality, which is totally invisible, and a subjective, green-tinged reality, which is visible but totally false. In this strange case the visible green reality would be more real and objective than the invisible reality.

WE: We can certainly agree with that. It seems that if the process of evolution had given the entire human race green lenses in their eyes, we would be completely justified in saying that reality is the green-tinged reality perceived by the human race. We would even be justified in claiming that there is no point in talking about any other reality. For what is the point of raising hypotheses about invisible realities?

KANT: Excellent! What, then, is the direction of fit?

WE: The direction of fit?

KANT: The fit between physical reality and human perception. Is it physical reality that caused the lenses of the people in the parable to be green, or is it the green lenses that caused physical reality to look green?

WE: Undoubtedly the green-tinged world was generated by the green lenses.

KANT: In that case don't you have to admit that it was external reality that was fitted to the structure of human vision?

WE: It does seem possible that reality could be influenced by the structure of human vision. But what is the moral of this parable?

KANT: The glasses in the parable are the a priori rules of arithmetic and geometry and the stipulations of causality. My thesis is that all the a priori rules are like glasses through which we perceive external reality.

WE: But how does this work?

KANT: These are not eyeglasses but mind-glasses. I think that our mind is absolutely subject to the rules of mathematics and geometry and to the two stipulations of causality: "Everything has a cause" and "Once a cause, always a cause." Thus we are unable to perceive or think about anything that would contradict these laws.

WE: That is, they are necessarily true. But we have already accepted that.

KANT: Be patient. . . . The parable of the glasses has a much wider significance: It follows from this thesis that we can never think or perceive anything that contradicts these a priori laws! For all our empirical information about our environment is fitted in advance to these rules, just as the picture that was seen through the green glasses was shifted toward green before it reached our consciousness.

WE: And what follows from this?

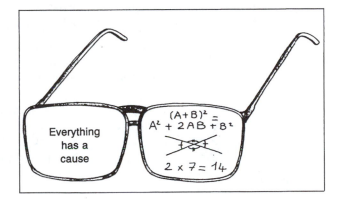

KANT: It follows that we are compelled to see the world as if it were subject to these a priori laws and operated accordingly, although we know that the actual source of the laws is in our minds.

Let's make this more concrete: Imagine once again that our eyes are covered by nonremovable glasses, but that instead of the glasses coloring the world green, they color it with "cause and effect," with numbers and lines, and make it seem to operate according to the law that "everything has a cause" and to the rules of geometry.

WE: It seems very implausible, but it's not logically impossible.

KANT: Not only is it possible, but it's very likely that that's the way things are. For there is no other way to explain why we are able to freely use the laws of arithmetic, geometry, and causality for the purposes of the empirical sciences.

WE: Okay, but there is still something that bothers us: How do you know that objective reality—which is not dependent on how we see it—is not totally different from our picture of it?

KANT: Let me repeat my argument: We know that certain laws are a priori laws of our reason, and that only through these laws are we able to perceive reality. Therefore we will never be faced with another reality that contradicts them.

What's the point, then, of speaking of "objective reality," independent of the phenomenal world as it appears to us, if we will never be able to see or even to imagine it? We must stipulate that the world of phenomena—that which our minds can grasp—is all there is.

WE: Is this what assures us that the a priori laws, like the law that "everything has a cause," are true laws of nature?

KANT: Precisely! This serves to resolve Hume's doubts in the previous chapter. We can do science to discover the laws of nature because we are able to make use of the a priori laws whose source is in our pure reason and which comprise the narrow base of the scientific pyramid.

We already saw, at the end of the previous chapter, how to use the a priori stipulations of causality combined with empirical observations to prove the law that "water boils at 100°C at atmospheric pressure." All other scientific laws can be proved in the same way.

This solves the problem we posed at the beginning of our discussion: "How is knowledge of the world possible?" It's possible because the foundation of knowledge and science is the a priori laws, that is, the laws inherent in our minds—laws whose very truth is derived from the fact that they are our mind-glasses, through which we see the world.

Thus the narrow base of Hume's inverted pyramid has been rescued, and science has been restored to its place in peace and security!

*

We've presented you with Kant's answer to Hume's question: The validity of empirical knowledge is not based on the laws of science but rather on the laws of pure reason.

The truth of these laws (the "a priori laws") is derived from the fact that we see reality through them. We deduce this from the fact that these laws are necessary presuppositions for all empirical knowledge. Therefore the information inherent in them is necessarily true; that is, it necessarily fits reality.

Thus there are two factors involved in the generation of reality or nature, rather than only one, as was previously believed:

The first factor is the external world, which provides the millions of impressions received by our senses: sounds, sights, smells, and the like.

The second factor is the structure of pure reason, which provides the highest and most comprehensive laws of reality: the laws of causality, arithmetic, and geometry.

When the impressions we grasp through our senses join with the a priori laws of our mind, a rich picture of the world is created. This picture synthesizes a rich variety of impressions and phenomena (whose source is in the external world) into a well-ordered structure (whose source is in the human mind).

We end with Kant's own words from his book *Prolegomena:* "There are many laws of nature that we can only know by means of experience; but conformity to the law in the connection of appearances—i.e., nature in general—we can get to know through no experience, because experience itself needs such laws, which lie a priori at the ground of its possibility. . . . The highest legislation of nature must lie in ourselves, i.e., in our understanding; and . . . we must not seek the universal laws of nature from nature by means of experience, but conversely. . . . The understanding does not draw its laws (a priori) from nature, but prescribes them to nature."

Further Reading for Part I

Parmenides

His book *On Truth* was written in verse, and only a few pages of it have survived. The following are two examples of the many books in which these pages can be read in English translation:
F. M. Conford, *Plato and Parmenides*. London, 1939/1969.
L. Taran, *Parmenides*. Princeton, 1965.

•For further interpretation of both Parmenides and Zeno, see:
G. S. Kirk and J. E. Raven, *The Presocratic Philosophers*. Cambridge, 1957, pp. 263–285 (Parmenides), and pp. 287–297 (Zeno).

•A brilliant and delightful presentation of Parmenides' fantastic theory may be found in Montgomery Furth's paper, "Elements of Eleatic Ontology." It opens with the premise, "It cannot be said that anything is not," and shows—with the help of some dialogue—how Parmenides' fantastic conclusion about "The One" is derived. It is recommended that the beginning reader skip Section 1, which is quite scholarly. The rest of the paper is most charming. It may be found in *Journal of the History of Philosophy, 6*, April 1968.

Descartes

His cardinal philosophical work is *Meditations on First Philosophy*. If you understood Chapter 3 of the present book, you should not have any difficulty understanding the original source. In addition to Descartes's search for the first absolute truth, the book contains three proofs of the existence of God, one proof of the reality of material objects, and some arguments for the distinction between the body and the soul. This tiny book has three advantages for the beginner: It's short, it's brilliant, and it's considered to be one of the most significant philosophical works ever written. One source of this work is the following:

E. S. Haldane and G. R. T. Ross, *The Philosophical Works of Descartes*, Vol. 1, Cambridge, 1911/1984, pp. 131–199.

Hume

Reading Hume's chief work, *A Treatise of Human Nature*, is not an easy task. I will therefore limit my recommendation to the following three sections from Book I, Part III, whose contents are discussed in our chapter on Hume: Sect. II, "Of probability, and of the idea of cause and effect"; Sect. III, "Why a cause is always necessary"; and Sect. XIV, "Of the idea of necessary connexion." One edition is *A Treatise of Human Nature*, Glasgow, 1739/1978.

A popular presentation of Hume's problem of induction, which is a natural outcome of his attack on causality, can be found in Chapter 6, "On Induction," of Bertrand Russell's book, *The Problems of Philosophy*. This book, which is a very lucid introduction to philosophy, also contains chapters on Berkeley's idealism (Chapter 4) and on Kant's epistemology (Chapter 8). One edition is *Problems of Philosophy*, Oxford, 1912.

Kant

His principal work in the field of epistemology is *The Critique of Pure Reason*, which makes difficult reading not only for beginners but even for seasoned philosophers. For those who wish to read an original work by this important philosopher, I recommend the shorter book called *Prologomena to Any Future Metaphysics*, which Kant wrote expressly for the purpose of making his philosophy more accessible. It should be noted, however, that what seems simpler to Kant does not necessarily seem so to others. One translation is that of P. G. Lucas, Manchester, 1953.

PART II
WHAT AM I?
THE SOUL-BODY PROBLEM

When philosophers ask themselves, "Who am I and what am I made of?" they are thinking of the "soul-body" problem, which is also known as the "mind-body" problem. Let's try to explain these concepts. By "body" we mean the human body, with all its components and systems—the atoms and molecules that make up the various cells: the nerve cells, the muscle cells, the bone cells; the different limbs and organs: feet, hands, heart, stomach. The body also includes, of course, the most complex of all organs, the brain.

Bodies are composed of various material elements, and of them alone. Thus, when we say "body" we are necessarily referring to something that, like all physical objects, takes up space and has mass. This analysis has the significant implication that our bodies (like all other material objects) operate only in accordance with the laws of physics and chemistry.

To complete the presentation of the "soul-body" problem we must explain the meaning of "soul." Yet here something strange occurs: Although it was easy to explain the concept of "body," the opposite applies to an explanation of "soul." Actually the only way we can say what this concept means is by contrasting it with "body": "Soul" means something that is not composed of material elements like the body, and some philosophers call it the "immaterial mind." Accordingly (and again in contrast with the body), the soul is not made up of parts and does not take up space. This analysis implies a significant conclusion about the soul: the soul is not compelled to operate according to the laws of physics and chemistry!

Many philosophers have addressed themselves to this issue. Their rich variety of solutions can be divided into three types:

I am a body

I am a body and a soul

I am a soul

61

1

I Am a Body:
The Materialist

The universe is made up of many varied materials. The trillions of stars clustered into millions of galaxies are nothing but great conglomerations of matter. Our entire earth is nothing but a massive concentration of billions of molecules and atoms organized in the shape of a ball and moving as one entity through space.

The mountains and rocks on the surface of the earth are also made of matter. Even the oceans and seas are nothing but a huge aggregation of water molecules, with a few percent of other materials.

That is the world. And what about me?

If the entire universe is made of matter, then I too, as a tiny part of the universe, am made of matter.

As a rational person I don't see any reason to assume that in all this enormous universe, made up entirely of matter, I should be an exception in being made up (partly or entirely) of soul. I find it natural to stipulate that the term "I" coincides with "my body"; that is, when I say "I" I refer to my body, and nothing else.

This answer to the question "What am I?" is called "materialism." The materialist world-picture bases the entire world, including man, on one substance alone: "Everything is matter" (or, in modern scientific terms, "everything is mass and energy"). We know that bodies exist, so why not assume that there are living bodies, and that people are one sort of body of this type?

Nevertheless, we feel that there are some issues the materialist must clarify, in order for us to be convinced of his thesis.

WE: Do you seriously mean to claim that man is nothing but a body, that is, that a person is equivalent to the collection of all his limbs and organs?

MATERIALIST: Precisely.

WE: Do you mean that just as a pile of gravel weighing a ton is a collection of millions of tiny stones, so a person is nothing more than a conglomeration of the millions of tiny cells that make up his body?

MATERIALIST: I see you understand my position. In my view they are all subject to the same laws: a pile of gravel, a person, a mountain, and everything else.

WE: But if a pile of gravel loses half its weight, isn't it now worth only half of what it was worth before?

MATERIALIST: Certainly.

WE: Then if a person loses an arm or a leg, or loses a great deal of weight, is he worth less as a person? Should we, as in the case of the gravel, say that his value as a person is half of what it was before? Should we count him as half a person?

MATERIALIST: Are you making fun of me? Will you also suggest that someone who has lost half his weight should get only half a vote in the elections, and other insane proposals of that sort?

WE: But if a person is nothing but a pile of cells, that is what we should say!

MATERIALIST: The root of this absurdity is not in my theory, but in your comparison of a human body to a heap of gravel. A heap of gravel is nothing but a collection of small units without any necessary order or form. But a human body is totally different. In the human body the placement of the cells and the connections among them and among the larger organs are of vital importance. I think it would be more fitting to compare the human body to a machine with many parts, such as a car. A car is nothing more than headlights, motor, frame, seats, wheels, and so on—but organized into a particular structure, and functioning in a particular way.

Similarly, the human body is also the totality of its parts: heart, lungs, limbs, brain, and the rest, but organized into a particular structure and functioning in a particular manner. Consider this yourselves: If a wheel is replaced in a car, or one of its doors is torn off, would you say that it is still the same car, or would you claim that it is less of a car than before?

WE: It's still the same car.

MATERIALIST: Then if a person loses one of his limbs or organs—say, an arm—we should compare this case to the case of a car that has lost a door. As long as the car fulfills the essential functions of a car, it is a car. Similarly for a person, even if part of his body is replaced or lost, he is still a person to the same extent as before, and the very same person!

WE: But let's say this poor person has not just lost an arm or a leg, but that some more important internal organs, such as the heart and kidneys, have been removed from his body, and foreign organs transplanted in their place.

MATERIALIST: This is very unpleasant, but I have some consolation for this person: in cars and airplanes as well it often happens that not only the wheels but also the engine is replaced. Now the function of the engine is similar to that of the heart, lungs, and kidneys in the human body. Nevertheless, even if the entire engine is replaced, wouldn't you generally say that it is still the same car or plane?

WE: Yes.

MATERIALIST: Then you should say the same in the unfortunate case of a heart or kidney transplant.

WE: But if a person could have a brain transplant, what would you say then? Would you still consider him the very same person?

MATERIALIST: Aha! You've just presented an excellent example for clarifying my point. For in a car as well, if the entire chassis is replaced, we would no longer say it's the same car. Rather, we would say that the parts of the original car have been assembled onto a new chassis, and that this has created a new car. Isn't that what people say?

WE: Yes.

MATERIALIST: This is because, in people as in cars, and in contrast to heaps of gravel, not all parts play the same role. Some components are "more characteristic" of the given object than others. Thus we say that most parts of a car are replaceable, but that the chassis is the one fixed part that distinguishes this car from others. In people too we can speak of a hierarchy of organs. Most limbs and organs are in principle replaceable without changing the person's identity. The brain is the exception. It is the crucial part for determining a person's identity.

Frankly, I don't see any difference in principle here between the bodies of cars and the bodies of people. Moreover, I don't see any principled difference between cars and human beings at all, except, of course, for the fact that cars do not contain anything that comes anywhere near the complexity and sophistication of one of man's organs—namely, the brain.

WE: That's true, but there is one principled difference: A car can perform only mechanical acts, whereas a person, in addition to performing mechanical acts like motions, can also think! Wasn't it Descartes who claimed that thinking is the fundamental attribute distinguishing human beings from all other objects?

MATERIALIST: Let's assume that's true. How is it relevant to our discussion?

WE: For then you have to explain how a material object which in your opinion is only a "huge collection of molecules and atoms" is able to think. Is it possible for matter to think?

MATERIALIST: In the past this seemed to be a matter of principle, but nowadays we know that machines are able to think and to perform calculations. I am speaking, of course, of the computer. No one imagines that computers have souls or anything similar—it's obvious that they are made only of matter, and we even know what sort of materials they are made of. Yet computers are able to perform the most complicated calculations extremely quickly; they are able to store huge quantities of information in a memorylike system and to access this information when needed—to play chess, for example, and to perform many other varied operations.

Why not assume, then, that the human mind is nothing but a sophisticated supercomputer? The analogy between man and machine will still hold, except that instead of an ordinary car we will compare him to a pilotless airplane fitted with a computer that gives orders to each of its parts, and pilots it along its planned course, just as the human mind gives orders to all parts of the body. And although the variety of actions supervised by the human mind is considerably broader than that of any computer or robot, still the very fact that robots exist proves beyond any doubt that a material object is capable of performing calculations and of making plans and altering them in accordance with changing situations. Such an object can be made entirely of matter, and there is no particular need to assume that it also has a soul.

WE: Your comparison between brain and computer sounds convincing as long as it's confined to the areas you mentioned—calculations, plans, and memory. But there is an area you didn't mention in your analogy—the area of emotions and desires. Is it conceivable, for instance, that a computer might want something? Or feel something?

MATERIALIST: And why not? For instance, when a robot is preparing his arms to pick up something from the floor, we can say that he wants to pick it up—just as we say about a person.

WE: It doesn't make sense that a robot should want something. It can't want or even intend anything, because material objects cannot want or intend. Your reasoning leads to an absurd conclusion: If the preparations made automatically by the robot prior to performing a certain action are like the desires and intentions of people, the same should be true of every object in nature that is about to do something. Why shouldn't we say, for example, that the black cloud approaching us "wants" or "intends" to rain upon us? Or that the boulder which is about to be dislodged and roll down the slope "intends" and "wants" to fall?

In our opinion, it is ridiculous to attribute intentions to any material objects whatsoever, even if they are as organized and complex as computers or brains. True, computers and brains can make calculations, but they can't want or intend, because they are made of pure matter, and matter can't want or intend anything.

MATERIALIST: I see your difficulty, but I can't accept your arguments. First of all, when you say that machines can't think or have desires because material objects can't do these things, you're begging the question; you're assuming the very thing you are trying to prove. The question of whether or not material objects can think or desire is precisely the issue at stake in our discussion.

Moreover, it seems to me that your fierce resistance to the obvious material nature of man stems from a psychological difficulty. There is a natural psychological difficulty in accepting the fact that human beings are not essentially different from everything else in nature—in recognizing that we, like all other objects, are absolutely subject to the laws of physics and chemistry.

WE: But there are also objective difficulties in trying to explain man with the assumption that everything is matter. How can you explain, for example, that we feel pain? Would you go so far as to suggest that matter is capable of feeling pain? And how could matter feel anger or pity?

MATERIALIST: The feeling of pain is nothing but the firing of neurons in several parts of the brain. When I feel pain in my hand, neurons are firing in certain groups of cells; when I feel pain in my foot there are neurons firing in other groups of cells, and similarly for all other pains. This is also true of feelings of anger, hatred, love, pity, and all the other emotions. For example, our anger about a particular event is a complex sequence of activation of various groups of cells in the brain. First, sensory cells pick up a description of the event, and memory cells interpret it as similar to events that have elicited anger in the past. Then the electrical activity of these groups of cells sends messages to other parts of the brain responsible for action, telling them to prepare for some activity expressing our anger. At the same time the brain sends chemical messages to other parts of the body, causing the hormonal changes that we sense as a tightening in the chest or other bodily sensations of anger.

Of course, these particular explanations of sensations may not be entirely accurate, and science is not yet capable of explaining and demonstrating how every thought and feeling is actually a kind of electrical activity in the brain. Nonetheless, there is a great deal of empirical evidence in favor of the assumption that this is what actually happens. I'm even willing to go out on a limb and make the following prediction: It won't be very long until we are able to explain more and more "mental phenomena" as physical processes in the brain.

2

I Am a Body and a Soul: The Dualist

DUALIST: Our discussion with the materialist supported the commonsense notion that I am a "body" no less than anything else in nature: cars, stars, molecules, and trees. Yet nothing at all was settled about the soul.

WE: But didn't the materialist show us very nicely how it's possible to explain all mental functions as functions of the body?

DUALIST: Actually, I still harbor some doubts about that. . . . But let's assume that he did prove what he had set out to prove—that it's possible to explain all the mental functions attributed to the soul as physicochemical phenomena of the material brain. Should that convince us to accept his materialist viewpoint?

WE: Why shouldn't it?

DUALIST: All he proved is that it might be possible to explain "mental functions" as functions of the body. But in order to convert us to the materialist view he must also show that this is the only possible explanation for desires, intentions, and emotions. Do you think he did that?

WE: It didn't amount to that. Still, his explanations seemed quite convincing.

DUALIST: But if a certain thing can be explained one way, does that rule out the possibility of a different explanation?

WE: Not automatically.

DUALIST: And how do you decide between two different explanations—actually, two different theories about the same subject?

WE: There are objective scientific criteria for the examination of different theories. We put the two theories to experimental tests until one of them is proved false and the other is verified and accepted as true—or at least as more acceptable than the alternative.

DUALIST: Well and good. And what experiment do you propose for this purpose? What experiment can determine which theory to accept and which to abandon?

WE: When you have told us what exactly your theory is, we'll try to think of an appropriate experiment for testing it.

DUALIST: My theory is called dualism. This means that man is made up of two basic components: one is the body, which is made of matter, and the other is the soul, which is totally nonmaterial and lacks all the characteristic features of matter. The soul does not take up space; it does not have any weight; it cannot be taken apart and put back together again; and the like. The combination of these two substances—the soul and the body—is what we call a human being.

WE: Well and good. All that's left now is to see who's right.

DUALIST: Excellent! But what will the test be?

WE: We'll design a scientific experiment, or even a series of experiments and tests, and we'll let the results determine which theory is preferable.

DUALIST: Good God! Haven't you understood my question?

WE: What question? What are you talking about?

DUALIST: I'll ask you again: What is this "scientific experiment"? What instruments will you use to perform the measurements?

Please don't repeat that you'll perform a "scientific experiment" and that you'll use "scientific measurement tools." Just be good enough to provide the details: Will you use a ruler, or weights and balances, or what?

WE: It seems that we'll need a variety of instruments. Perhaps it would be better to consult a scientist before giving a detailed answer about such a matter.

DUALIST: Let's try to clarify the matter ourselves. I'm convinced that we can make some progress even without consulting a scientist. Tell me, aren't we discussing theories pertaining to a specific problem?

WE: Of course.

DUALIST: And what is it called?

WE: The soul-body problem.

DUALIST: Thus we are confronted with two distinct theories: one claiming that only bodies exist, and the other that a nonmaterial mind, or a soul, exists as well.

WE: True.

DUALIST: And, in principle, when we perform a scientific experiment to observe the human body, can't we use the same instruments used for the examination of other material objects?

WE: Of course.

DUALIST: That is, to measure the body we can use tape measures, balances, microscopes, electrical resistance meters, X rays, and similar instruments?

WE: That's right.

DUALIST: And how can you measure the soul?

WE: Perhaps we can use some sort of energy meter, if there is such a thing. Or perhaps some radiation meter? This sort of instrument might help us to find out whether souls exist, and perhaps even measure their energy or radiation.

DUALIST: But ever since the 1920s, when Einstein came out with his formula $e = mc^2$, stating that energy (e) and mass (m) are two sides of the same coin, we've known that energy is only another form of matter.

WE: Yes, we heard about that.

DUALIST: Yet when I presented the dualist approach I emphasized that the term ''soul'' means something immaterial, that is, something that is not made of matter.

WE: True.

DUALIST: Hence the soul (at least in the ordinary sense of this word) is not energy, since energy is only a different form of matter, isn't it?

WE: If that is the case it will be quite hard to detect it.

DUALIST: ''Quite hard?'' It's totally impossible. If the soul is immaterial by definition, it can never be measured by instruments or observed by the senses. Therefore, no scientific experiment can ever be devised that will confirm or refute its existence. It follows that the determination of which of the two theories is superior is a totally unscientific issue.

All of a sudden, while we are still trying to understand the dualist's argument, the materialist intervenes: I see that my friend the dualist has led you into a blind alley by offering this subtle argument: that you will never be able to decide between the two theories, because one of them—the dualist theory—cannot be scientifically tested. Isn't that the essence of his claim?

WE: That's a good summary.

MATERIALIST: Well, I've known him for a long time. . . . Dualists are sharp and cunning, like most metaphysicians. Since they deal with what is beyond the limits of science and sense, they cannot justify their ideas scientifically, and so they use their slyness and their sharp tongues as their weapons. When dealing with such people you have to be very cautious of accepting their views. See for yourself: Just now the dualist has almost led you to agree that the discussion has ended in a draw—just when you've reached the crucial point. The point you've now reached is the most appropriate point for deciding between the two rival theories.

DUALIST: But I thought, Mr. Materialist, that science is your only criterion for deciding between theories.

MATERIALIST: And you thought right, my dear friend.

DUALIST: In that case, I don't see how you can decide that materialism is preferable to dualism, since you admit that the latter can't be scientifically tested.

MATERIALIST: That's exactly why, my friend!

WE: What do you mean?

MATERIALIST: I claim that materialism is preferable to dualism because dualism cannot be scientifically described or tested! Look—if we assume that these two theories are equivalent in every other respect, which of course I don't believe for a minute, the only aspect that would be left for comparing them would be their accessibility to science. Now, according to the dualist approach, we will never be able to thoroughly describe and investigate the nature of man, because the soul will always remain out of our reach. According to the materialist view, on the other hand, it is possible and even probable that someday we will be able to give a full scientific account of human nature and explain all human actions using scientific terminology. The conclusion is clear: The acceptance of dualism means a dead end in our understanding of man, since if we accept it we can say nothing more. The adoption of the materialist solution, on the other hand, will encourage us to continue investigating man and thus we will gain as much knowledge as possible. It's clear, then, that the materialist theory is scientifically preferable to dualism.

WE: Well, Mr. Dualist, it seems that if we will adopt this pragmatic approach we might get out of the blind alley we are stuck in.

DUALIST: If you will permit me to summarize what my friend the materialist has just said, this is the gist of his argument: The dualist theory is the inferior one precisely because it is impossible to perform any scientific experiment that might refute it.

MATERIALIST: You've changed my formulation somewhat, but that is definitely the essence of what I said. I prefer the materialist approach precisely because it can be investigated by scientific experiments and observations.

DUALIST: If so, the issue is worthy of clarification.

MATERIALIST: What do you mean?

DUALIST: I don't see how the materialist approach is scientifically accessible.

MATERIALIST: Well, if human beings are made of matter—and of matter alone—then, like other material objects, they can be tested and measured scientifically.

DUALIST: That's perfectly true. But how does it affect our discussion?

MATERIALIST: Well, I already demonstrated in the previous chapter that according to the materialist approach every piece of knowledge, every feeling, every sensation are all specific arrangements of materials in the brain, or particular instances of electrical and chemical activity. Therefore all this human activity is accessible to research and observation.

DUALIST: Once again you are not speaking to the point. The scientific measurability of our bodies is obvious to one and all. But the human body is not the materialist theory, and they are not equally testable. So I still don't see how the materialist theory is scientifically accessible.

MATERIALIST: But it's obvious. No one can claim that the dualist theory has the slightest link with science or with a scientific world-view. In contrast, it's almost self-evident that a theory dealing with an object that can be scientifically investigated—which is the sort of theory materialism is—has a strong link with science, or at least with the scientific world-view.

Here the dualist interrupts angrily: And I contend that materialism is an unscientific metaphysical theory no less than dualism!

MATERIALIST: Strong words! Next you will accuse me of being a metaphysician!

DUALIST: Exactly! That's what I claim. Answer me: Isn't materialism opposed to dualism in that it denies the existence of the soul?

MATERIALIST: Good God! How far will you go to try to connect me with the concept of a soul? All I claim is that human beings are material objects. As for souls, I'm totally uninterested in them.

DUALIST: But isn't your assertion that "man is a body" equivalent to the assertion that "man is a body and not a soul?" Do you think that there may be a soul too? Or that it's plausible that there might be?

MATERIALIST: Okay! "Man is a body"—and for you, my dear friend, I add: And not a soul!

DUALIST: But we've agreed that science has nothing to say about the soul, haven't we? That it can neither confirm nor refute its existence?

MATERIALIST: True.

DUALIST: But in order for materialism to be scientifically testable and refutable, it must be possible for science to prove one of the following: Either that there is no soul, thus supporting materialism; or that there *is* a soul, thus refuting it.

Since the materialist remained gloomily silent, we answered instead of him: All right, please proceed.

DUALIST: And since science cannot prove either of these two propositions, it follows that science can neither support nor refute either dualism or materialism.

WE: That seems to emerge from our discussion.

DUALIST: Therefore materialism is a metaphysical theory to precisely the same extent as dualism; and you, Mr. Materialist, are just as much a metaphysician as I am!

WE: It seems that you're right in claiming that the soul-body problem is not a scientific issue at all, but rather a metaphysical problem. But you still haven't given us any good reason to accept dualism and to believe that the existence of souls is necessary.

DUALIST: Now that we've shown that science is irrelevant and demonstrated that the soul-body problem is a purely metaphysical problem, the time has come to clarify it philosophically. But first answer this: What makes you so sure of the existence of material objects and bodies?

WE: Experience! We constantly experience the existence of such objects in our surroundings, including the existence of our own bodies. We see, hear, and bump into various objects all day long.

DUALIST: And isn't the same thing true of the soul? That is, if we could somehow verify its existence, wouldn't it also be through some experience that attests to it?

WE: So it would seem. But it's impossible for there to be any such experience.

DUALIST: Impossible?

WE: Have you forgotten what you said just a moment ago? You established with certainty, and with the agreement of everyone here, that there is no scientific experiment that could support or refute the idea of the existence of souls. And your argument was that we are not capable of sensing the immaterial with any of our five senses!

DUALIST: And I still hold to that assertion of mine.

WE: Then how can you speak of experience?

DUALIST: Well, what about a nonsensory experience?

WE: Extrasensory perception? Is that what you're talking about?

DUALIST: Don't you agree that things like love, hate, affection, and the like really exist?

WE: Yes.

DUALIST: And how do you know about the existence of love,

hate, and the like? After all, neither you nor anyone else has ever perceived them by means of the senses.

WE: And that's why their existence is really doubtful! A final analysis might show that none of them has an independent existence. It might show that love and hate are, as the materialist claimed, nothing more than certain physical states in our brains.

DUALIST: I'm not asking you right now what love and hate are, whether they're material or immaterial. I'm only asking you—and I am still waiting for your answer—how you know they exist.

WE: We feel them.

DUALIST: Do you feel their existence by means of your five senses? Or somehow independently of the senses?

WE: If you are asking how people come to know about other people's feelings of love and hate, then it seems to us that they must enlist the aid of the senses. But if you mean to ask how people find out what their own feelings are, then we must answer that they do not perceive them by means of their senses.

DUALIST: Thus there exists extrasensory experience?

WE: Yes.

DUALIST: And since this experience is not sensory, it is necessarily not experience of a scientific nature.

WE: Not if you are talking about the private experience of each person in his or her own private world.

DUALIST: And what do you say about "will"? How do I know that I want something, that is, that a certain desire exists within me? Do I find out about my desires through my senses, or in some other way?

WE: Some other way.

DUALIST: And isn't matter defined in part as what is perceived, or can in principle be perceived, by the senses?

WE: Yes.

DUALIST: And is it conceivable that the existence of any material object could be grasped without the mediation of the senses?

WE: That's absolutely impossible.

DUALIST: And this implies the following: that love and hate, as well as all other feelings and desires, are not material, since they can sometimes be grasped without the mediation of the senses.

WE: That's not so clear. For if the materialist is correct in assuming that all emotions are actually physical states of the brain, then it would be possible to perceive their existence via our senses, if we only knew how to peek into our brains and how to identify the physical expression of each feeling and belief. If we can achieve this, we will be able to attach electrodes to people's brains and see their loves and desires as they occur.

DUALIST: If the materialist is right. Nevertheless, even if this were possible, it would still not obscure the fact that people can usually recognize their own feelings without recourse to their senses.

WE: We've already agreed on that.

DUALIST: And haven't we also agreed that there can be no material object that could be perceived in an extrasensory way?

WE: We've agreed to that as well. But still, isn't it possible that it will turn out at some future date that feelings and desires are merely physical brain states, and then . . .

DUALIST: Never! If these were physical states, then it would never be possible to be aware of them without the use of our senses. The fact that we are aware of their existence without the mediation of our senses proves that they can never be fully identified with any brain states, because physical states cannot be recognized in an extrasensory way, whereas these states can.

WE: All right. We must agree that feelings, desires, beliefs, and the like definitely exist, but their essence is not merely material and they are not just physical states of some sort.

DUALIST: Excellent; we've already made great progress, as we've proved the existence of nonmaterial things. From this point on, the path to the soul is not very far. Please answer this question: Is it possible for a person to observe and be aware of the desires and feelings of others in the same direct way that they themselves are aware of them—that is, without the assistance of the senses?

WE: Of course not. Every person has his private consciousness and is directly aware only of his own desires and emotions. As to the desires and emotions of other people, one can only figure them out by looking at them and at their behavior, or by listening to what they say—that is, only by means of the senses.

DUALIST: We agree, then, that people are confronted with two distinct worlds. One is the public physical world that is grasped by the senses. In principle, all its parts are open to observation by everyone. This is the world that is dealt with by science; and my body, including my brain, belongs to this public domain.

The second world confronting each of us is one's own private domain, which includes all the things that a person is aware of directly, in an unmediated way—his or her own desires, emotions, and beliefs.

Although the existence of each person's emotions, thoughts, and desires is a fact—for example, it is a fact that I now want a certain thing—these facts are directly available only to their owners. Of course, one can draw conclusions about other people's feelings, but only indirectly and never with absolute certainty.

WE: All very well, as we've already agreed that there are things like desires and emotions that we know about without the use of the senses. But how do we know that the existence of emotions and desires is evidence for the existence of a soul that generates or controls them?

DUALIST: We discover a certain order and coordination among our many and various feelings, desires, and thoughts. This order undoubtedly stems from the fact that they have one source—that is, that they are all generated by or connected with some one thing—which we call a "soul."

WE: This is a very nice hypothesis, but it is only a hypothesis. For we have direct experience—unmediated experience, as you call it—of the existence of our feelings and thoughts. But we do not have any direct experience of the existence of a soul that connects them all.

DUALIST: And what about the existence of objects?

WE: We have direct experience of the existence of objects. We see, hear, and touch them all the time.

DUALIST: We hear sound waves; we see and touch the outer surfaces of things, and we see the light they reflect. You can therefore say that there are light waves, sounds, and feelings of touch; but how do you know that there is one object behind all the sensations that we experience from, for example, this wooden table?

WE: Because our sensations of touch and sight concerning the table fit well with each other. After all, how could they fit so well if they didn't all originate from the same particular object?

DUALIST: That seems very logical to me. You're right in judging that what lies behind our various sensations, which coordinate so well with one another, should be called an object or a body. That is, the very existence of various coordinated perceptions is excellent proof of the existence of objects.

WE: And souls?

DUALIST: The same reasoning applies to souls as well. After all, every one of us (I hope) has unmediated consciousness of his or her desires, thoughts, and feelings at various times, and there is a degree of coordination among all of these. From this it follows that all these immaterial phenomena are included in or connected with one unifying factor, called the "soul."

If our sensory experience of a table or any other material object is sufficient evidence that that particular object exists—and I believe that this is the case—then, by the same reasoning, our extra-sensory experience of feelings and beliefs is sufficient evidence for the existence of the thing that unifies them—in other words, the existence of the soul.

3

I Am a Soul: Idealism

When someone claims that he is a "soul," it sounds rather odd. The belief in souls is usually associated with the belief in life after death or reincarnation. Such beliefs are generally related to religion and seem to most of us both unscientific and contradictory to common sense.

The philosopher George Berkeley (who was also a bishop) was an ardent advocate of common sense. Thus he vigorously attacked superstitions and prejudices.

But what is a prejudice? According to Berkeley, it is an idea that people take to be so obviously true that there is no need to prove it. In order to do battle against such beliefs or prejudices, and to induce people to reexamine them, Berkeley wrote a book called *The Principles of Human Knowledge*. Right at the beginning he wrote:

> Because the tenet of the existence of Matter seems to have taken so deep a root in the mind of philosophers, and draws after it so many ill consequences, I choose rather to be thought prolix and tedious than omit anything that might conduce to the full discovery and extirpation of that prejudice.[1]

No, this is not an error; this is indeed what Berkeley wrote, black on white! Berkeley is accusing us of being prejudiced because of our belief in the existence of matter!

Because of our belief? Are you, a bishop, accusing us of blind belief? Doesn't science confirm the reality of materials and bodies by investigating them continually?

"The burden of proof," says Berkeley, "is on you. If the belief in material objects is not a prejudice, what is your proof of it?"

1. This paragraph was omitted in later editions.

We are shocked at this accusation, and the sense of ridicule we felt disappears. Can we prove (even in principle) the existence of material objects?

Nevertheless, we feel insulted that an Irish bishop who lived some three hundred years ago should make fun of us and leave us speechless. Let's try to answer him simply.

WE: We see them with our own eyes.

BERKELEY: You see? And that's all you can say in your defense? What does it mean that you "see"? What value is there in sight?

WE: We see objects. We see them so often and for so long that we are sure we can't be mistaken about them.

BERKELEY: This is not a proof, only an excuse.

WE: Why an excuse?

BERKELEY: Is this a good proof—seeing something many times?

WE: It's generally accepted as such.

BERKELEY: And does something become true because you see it many times? I, for example, have put spoons in glasses of tea many times, and then seen them appear bent. Does that make me a spoon-bender? Is the appearance of the spoon a conclusive proof that it is really bent?

WE: No.

BERKELEY: And since you live in the twentieth century, you undoubtedly go to the movies and see films?

WE: Yes, quite often.

BERKELEY: And when you see there, as you say, "with your own eyes," an ape-monster as tall as a skyscraper, do you believe that this creature is real?

WE: We're not that naive.

BERKELEY: Then the fact that "we see" material objects all the time is not proof enough that they really exist.

WE: We admit that it's not a proof, at least not a conclusive one.

At this point Berkeley seems quite pleased with himself. What he doesn't know (after all, he lived some three hundred years ago) is that we have a "secret weapon" at our disposal which we can use to launch our counteroffensive. This weapon is the modern scientific theory of light waves.

WE: Bishop Berkeley, do you know how we really see objects?

BERKELEY: Do you mean ''with our eyes''?

WE: Oh, no! It's much more complicated than that. Science has proved that light rays are reflected from all sorts of material objects, and that these rays disperse at tremendous speed in every direction. When they hit our retina, and the image is transformed into electrical impulses and carried to the visual center, then seeing takes place.

BERKELEY: Fine. But why should we care about these light rays?

WE: They constitute our proof! Listen: We agree with you that not everything we see must exist in reality. We admit that in many cases our sight can deceive us, as in the case of the bent spoon in the glass or of King Kong on the movie screen. We are even willing to admit that it's often difficult to know whether things actually are the way they look.

Yet there's one thing we can't agree with! For even if we are mistaken about what we have seen, it's still clear that some-thing—and it doesn't matter exactly what—*something* has to be there! For it's absolutely certain that the light waves that reach our eyes are being reflected from some object.

BERKELEY: It's not obvious to me.

WE: Let's focus on the film example for a moment. Imagine that King Kong appears before our eyes.

BERKELEY: Very well.

WE: And in objective reality, as we all agree, King Kong does not exist?

BERKELEY: Definitely not.

WE: But what about the screen on which King Kong's picture is projected? At least the screen and the picture must truly exist, as it is the picture that reflects the light waves into our eyes.

BERKELEY: Why?

WE: But it's obvious!

BERKELEY: And how do you know there really is a screen?

WE: We see it! Oh, we're sorry . . . that isn't a good answer; . . . we've already admitted that seeing doesn't prove that the thing we're seeing actually exists . . .

Okay, Berkeley, let's forget the screen, since we'll never be able to prove its existence. Now we're no longer so sure that there is a screen, and we're not so sure of the existence of objects that reflect light into our eyes. But there's one thing you still can't deny—the existence of light waves themselves.

BERKELEY: Why not?

WE: For even if they're not reflected by anything, the waves themselves must exist. After all, we see them directly, and if they did not exist and did not hit our eyes, vision would not be possible. We would not even be able to see illusions like King Kong.

BERKELEY: I don't accept that.

WE: But it's a decisive proof!

BERKELEY: No, it's not, since I can still ask how you know that there are "light waves."

WE: But we already told you that we see them . . . Oh, sorry . . . "see" isn't right. . . . How can we put it? . . . They impinge upon our eyes!

BERKELEY: And how do you know?

WE: Because we see the . . . uh . . . uh . . . What do we actually see? . . . Well, it's not so important *what* we see. The important thing is that there are light waves, or something else that impinges on our eyes when we see, and it doesn't matter what exactly it is.

BERKELEY: And whenever you "see" anything, does something impinge on your eyes? And when you are asleep, and your eyes are closed, do light waves still reach the retinas of your eyes?

WE: No.

BERKELEY: But don't we often dream, and see things in our dreams?

WE: Yes.

BERKELEY: Here I simply must repeat the words of our master Descartes: "There are no certain indications by which we may clearly distinguish between the state of wakefulness and that of sleep." Or do you have such an indication in mind?

WE: No.

BERKELEY: And when you see various objects in your dreams, do these objects truly exist?

WE: No.

BERKELEY: And what about the light waves that impinge upon your eyes and cause you to see? Do they certainly exist?

WE: Not in that case.

BERKELEY: Then this is evidence for sight without light!

WE: But in a dream we don't really see. All that happens is that we form certain visual images.

BERKELEY: Fine. And to this I add that throughout our lives we generate many thoughts and ideas, some visual and some not. Yet beyond them there is nothing. Material objects and bodies do not objectively exist, but are all the fruit of our mind.

Thus if you ask me about the sights, sounds, and other sensations that are received by our sense organs, this is my response: All these are no more than ideas in our minds. It is neither necessary nor useful to assume the existence of an external material world lying beyond our experience.

WE: Wait a second—what about our own bodies?

BERKELEY: There are no bodies. We are no different in this respect from the rest of the world. What seems to us as our body is only a collection of ideas and impressions.

*

People who claim, like Berkeley, that there are no material objects in the world, but that the entire world is a collection of souls with their thoughts and ideas, are called philosophical "idealists." This is not the common usage of the term "idealists"; here it denotes a philosophical school that casts doubt on the existence of material objects and believes that minds and ideas alone exist. Here are some excerpts from Berkeley's book that express this unusual view:

> It is indeed an opinion strangely prevailing amongst men, that houses, mountains, rivers, and, in a word, all sensible objects, have an existence, natural or real, distinct from their being perceived by the understanding. . . . But though it were possible that solid, figured, moveable substances may exist without the mind, corresponding to the ideas we have of bodies, yet how is it possible for us to know this?
>
> As for our senses—they do not [directly] inform us that things exist without the mind, or unperceived. . . . This the Materialists themselves acknowledge. . . . [And] what reason can induce us to believe the existence of bodies without mind, from what we perceive, since the very patrons of Matter themselves do not pretend there is any *necessary* connexion betwixt them and our ideas?
>
> I say it is granted on all hands—and what happens in dreams, frenzies, and the like, puts it beyond dispute— that it is possible we might be affected with all the ideas we have now, though there were no bodies existing. Hence it is evident [that] the supposition of external bodies is not necessary for the producing of our ideas. . . . In short, if there were external bodies, it is impossible we should ever come to know it; and if there were not, we

might have the very same reasons to think there were that we have now.

In summary, according to Berkeley the entire world consists of minds and their thoughts, with nothing beyond them. Even if we suppose that there is something like objects (including our own bodies) beyond our thoughts and imaginings, we will never be able to prove it. Why is this so?

Because we can never use anything but the thoughts and ideas, and not the objects themselves. What appears to us is not the tree or the house or the person, but perceptions grasped by our minds of the tree, the house, or the person; and how can we know about the existence of anything beyond the visual, auditory, and tactile sensations in our minds?

Perhaps some of us may try to refute Berkeley's extreme view by the use of scientific knowledge. After all, if science can prove so many things, it will surely be easy for it to demonstrate Berkeley's error as well.

But the scientists' response is liable to disappoint us: Science, they say, does not deal with unprovable things, but only with things or hypotheses that it can prove. After all, all of scientific knowledge is gained through the use of the senses. Even when the scientist makes use of measuring instruments, he uses them with the mediation of his senses, whose impressions are the instrument of all scientific cognition. Thus when Berkeley claims, as a general principle, that "the senses are incapable of demonstrating the existence of bodies and matter," the scientist cannot argue with him. The controversy about the significance of the senses is a principled controversy, and science, by its very nature, cannot deal with such matters.

But isn't science based on the idea that there are physical bodies and objects? Yes, say the scientists, but this is an unprovable assumption, an axiom that there is no point in doubting.

And the reader should note that the terms "assumption" and "axiomatic idea" are, after all, nothing but synonyms for the term with which we began this chapter: "prejudice."

Further Reading for Part II

Plato

The dualistic viewpoint, according to which man is a combination of body and soul, is presented in a lively and powerful manner by Plato. I especially recommend the dialogue "Phaedo," extensive parts of which are devoted to a discussion by Socrates and his friends about the existence of the soul, life after death, and the mutual relationship between the body and the soul. This dialogue also deals with epistemology, and it presents the theory of "remembering" (which is also presented in the dialogue "Meno") and the theory of ideas. A classic English translation of *The Dialogues of Plato*, which includes "Phaedo," is that of B. Jowett, New York, 1973.

Berkeley

His principal book is *The Principles of Human Knowledge*, where he sets out his pure empiricist outlook. The "motto" of the book is the proposition that "to be is to be perceived." From this it follows that matter does not exist, since it is not matter itself but only perceptions that are perceived. The book is extremely readable; I once heard someone claim that it is "the simplest of all philosophical books." The main arguments are concentrated in Paragraphs 2–24 and 145–149. This book may be found in a collection of Berkeley's writings entitled, *Principles, Dialogues and Philosophical Correspondence*, Indianapolis, 1966.

General Discussions

•A readable book entirely devoted to the soul-body problem is Keith Campbell's *Body and Mind*, London, 1970, which presents a wide variety of modern "solutions" to the problem.

•Very clear, and therefore highly recommended, is R. Taylor's presentation of the problem in his book *Metaphysics*, Prentice-Hall, 1974, Chapters 2–4.

•An interesting discussion of this problem in the form of a real dialogue is the following: K. R. Popper and J. C. Eccles, *The Self and Its Brain*, Berlin: Springer, 1977.

PART III

DETERMINISM, FREEDOM, AND WILL

Our feeling of free will, the sensation that we are capable of actively influencing the world and especially our own lives, is one of our basic experiences. It gives us a feeling of uniqueness and superiority, as it makes us the only entities in the world whose history, state, and behavior are not predetermined, but are affected, at least to some degree, by our will.

It must be emphasized that we do not perceive this will of ours as a type of animal instinct. To the contrary, we take it to be a genuine free will. The owners of such a thing are able to determine their own behavior in the next instant. Therefore we see this behavior, as well as our more distant future, not as fully determined by inanimate nature but rather as something that is up to us to decide about and shape.

According to what? According to our will and desires.

Descartes taught us in Chapter 3 of Part I that our possession of free will is one of the most basic and certain facts we can know, almost like our certainty that we are thinking beings. This fact belongs to the "private domain" of cognition, and its existence cannot be doubted. This is because no observational fact can refute the existence of our private consciousness. Therefore it seems that neither observational data nor scientific considerations can contradict this fundamental fact, which is based on the self-reflection of each human being.

All the same, our intention in this part of the book is to consider this fact, and even to cast some doubt on it. This will be done in two separate discussions on the issue of free will:

1. The first discussion is a dialogue in which we meet a determinist who discusses free will independently of its connection with human beings.

The determinist tries to show that "free will" cannot be reconciled with the world. He argues that it is impossible for such a thing to exist, as it would lead to serious contradictions.

But how can this be demonstrated? In the determinist's opinion one of the following possibilities must be the case:

The world follows the laws of causality.

There is no causality in the world.

"I claim," says the determinist, "that it doesn't matter which of these views we adopt, because each of them contradicts the possibility of free will."

2. The second discussion is an imaginary dialogue in which Socrates and his friends consider the possibility that the will is free. This dialogue is not directly based on a specific Platonic dialogue; I attempted to give Socrates only such lines of reasoning as maintain his basic trends of thought on this topic. Socrates, who accepts the existence of the will, questions the concept of freedom:

What is the meaning of the "freedom" we attribute to ourselves? Is man free to want anything he wants to want?

1

Determinism and Free Will

DETERMINIST: Let's begin our discussion by accepting the general assumption that "everything has a cause," ignoring Hume's philosophical doubts on this topic.

LIBERTARIAN: I'm happy to accept it, since I must admit that if I had not read Hume's strange philosophical thesis it would never have entered my mind to cast doubt on such a basic assumption.

DETERMINIST: Then let's try to encompass the entire universe in our minds. Let's try to consider all parts of the universe—from the great to the small, from the stars and galaxies to the tiniest atoms—and let's ask: Is the universe at this moment in a definite state?

LIBERTARIAN: What do you mean?

DETERMINIST: Since each tiny particle of the universe is now in a definite place, and has a definite weight, and is moving in a definite direction with a definite speed, we may conclude that the entire universe, which is the collection of all these particles, is itself in a definite state at the present moment.

LIBERTARIAN: Of course, everything that exists must exist in a certain state while in existence, and this includes the universe as a whole.

On the other hand, we must keep in mind that the universe is so large and made up of so many parts and particles that we'll never discover its exact state. In order to do that we would have to find out the state and location of every elementary particle among all the trillions of particles comprising the universe, which is an impossible task.

DETERMINIST: I didn't ask for the exact state of the universe, but only for your agreement that it is always in such a state.

LIBERTARIAN: And I do agree.

DETERMINIST: In that case, the time has come to ask: What caused the universe to be in its present definite state?

LIBERTARIAN: You don't seriously expect me to answer that question, do you? In order to do so I would need to investigate what caused each of the trillions of particles in the universe to be in its present state, and I've just explained why this is impossible.

DETERMINIST: But I didn't ask you about each particle separately. I'm not looking for trillions of causes. What I'm looking for is a single answer that will embrace the entire universe. I'm asking for a general definition of the cause of its being in its present state.

LIBERTARIAN: This is a question I can deal with. The cause of the present state of the universe is its precise state at the previous moment.

DETERMINIST: Excellent. And what caused universe's state at that "previous moment"?

LIBERTARIAN: That is quite clear. The state of the universe at any specific moment is the direct and exclusive effect of its state at the previous moment, and its state at the previous moment is the direct and exclusive effect of its state at the moment before that, and so on and so forth.

DETERMINIST: You see, when we assume that "everything has a cause"—that the universe functions according to the laws of causality—then it turns out that each of its states is fully determined by its previous states. This implies that all the events that have ever occurred were actually predetermined billions of years ago. Thus there can't be any freedom and nothing is free.

LIBERTARIAN: That's an interesting theory.

DETERMINIST: It's called the "determinant theory," or "determinism."

LIBERTARIAN: But do you really believe that the present state of everything whatsoever was determined billions of years ago?

DETERMINIST: Precisely! Take the moon, for example: I claim that its present state—its position at a certain distance from the earth, its motion in a certain direction at a certain speed—is a necessary state which was determined a long time ago. If the moon's future location were not fully determined by its present state, scientists would not be able to calculate it precisely enough to send a spaceship there.

LIBERTARIAN: But what about the sudden eruptions of volcanoes and the unpredictable occurrences of earthquakes, every wave in the sea and every gust of air? Are all these predetermined?

DETERMINIST: Of course. And not only all of these, but also all the actions and thoughts of human beings—all are predetermined and must necessarily have occurred just as they have occurred, and as they will occur in the future. For according to determinism, the birth and growth of each individual human being, not to speak of the evolution of the human species, were and are determined by the state of the universe. After all, the universe includes everyone's parents as well as their physical and social environment.

LIBERTARIAN: I can't accept your last assertion. I don't believe that determinism applies to human beings.

DETERMINIST: Why not? What sense is there in claiming that determinism is true of the entire universe, except for one particular kind of thing, namely, human beings?

LIBERTARIAN: Well, I have two arguments against the application of determinism to human beings.

DETERMINIST: And what are they?

LIBERTARIAN: First, your determinism seems to be based on the materialist assumption that the world is made up only of particles of matter which operate according to the mechanistic laws of physics. I, on the other hand, tend to the belief that there are also immaterial entities such as souls, and this contradicts the tenets of determinism.

Second, my ability to influence the actions I will perform next seems to be an undeniable fact; it's clear, for example, that the act of raising my right hand in a moment was not determined millions of years ago; rather, I and I alone will have decided whether or not to perform it.

DETERMINIST: Let's consider these arguments in order. First, you must clarify your first argument: What does the existence of souls have to do with determinism?

LIBERTARIAN: If there are souls, then it's a mistake to speak of "the precise state of the universe at every moment."

DETERMINIST: Why?

LIBERTARIAN: Because their very definition as "immaterial entities" excludes souls from having a precise mass or a precise location in space. In short, no "precise state" applies to them.

DETERMINIST: Obviously, if there are immaterial entities, then they do not possess the features of matter. But then mustn't they have some features of their own, other than location or mass?

LIBERTARIAN: Of course. Everything must have some kind of features. You probably know that believers in the existence of souls ascribe all sorts of features to them, some of them indeed quite odd.

DETERMINIST: Then they will surely agree that at every moment each soul has some specific content and definite features—for example, its aspirations, various feelings at varying intensities, and the like?

LIBERTARIAN: I suppose they would agree to this.

DETERMINIST: Thus, if souls exist, then is each soul also in a definite state at each and every moment?

LIBERTARIAN: It seems necessary.

DETERMINIST: Then even though you assume the existence of immaterial substances, this should not weaken our previous conclusion: that the universe, with all its components, is in a specific state at every moment, a state caused by its previous states.

LIBERTARIAN: Good God! I always thought that determinism was associated with the view that the world is made up only of matter, and that it operates according to the laws of physics. I thought that determinism was actually derived from materialism.

DETERMINIST: That's a widespread error. I do not see any association between the two theses: Determinism does not follow from the premises that the world is made entirely of matter and that all actions are determined by physical laws.

Determinism follows from a more economical premise: Every action is *caused*. It makes no difference to determinism what the laws are according to which actions take place—whether they are physical laws or psychological laws, or perhaps even esthetic principles. For my part, these laws can even be the laws of the transmigration of souls as they are described by Hindus. As long as we accept the stipulation that "everything has a cause," it follows from this, and from this alone, that all states of the universe have been predetermined.

LIBERTARIAN: Your argument is really impressive. But what do you have to say about my second problem?

DETERMINIST: Please remind us what it is.

LIBERTARIAN: That one of the most established facts about human beings is our ability to influence our own actions. For example, if I may be permitted to refer to myself, it is up to me to decide whether or not to raise my hand in a moment.

DETERMINIST: And according to what will you decide?

LIBERTARIAN: According to my will, I have the freedom to want either to do it or not to do it.

DETERMINIST: You claim, then, that desires exist?

LIBERTARIAN: Of course.

DETERMINIST: Then these desires are part of the universe, and so the stipulations of causality must apply to them too; for you surely remember that at the beginning of our discussion we agreed to stipulate that "everything has a cause."

LIBERTARIAN: That's what we agreed.

DETERMINIST: And this agreement implies that every desire is the result of something?

LIBERTARIAN: Yes, according to this stipulation.

DETERMINIST: The result of the state of the universe at the previous moment?

LIBERTARIAN: Why? A present desire may be, at least in principle, the continuation or outcome of a previous desire.

DETERMINIST: That's very true. But isn't this "previous desire" also an integral part of the state of the universe?

LIBERTARIAN: Yes.

DETERMINIST: Then the case where some present desire stems from a previous desire is included in the statement you rejected: that the present desire is the result of the previous state of the universe.

LIBERTARIAN: Then I have nothing more to say.

DETERMINIST: And what about the case where you wanted to raise your right hand? Can't we say that not only the act of raising your hand, but also the very formation of the desire to raise it, was predetermined billions of years ago?

LIBERTARIAN: It seems so, if we maintain your original premise that "everything has a cause."

DETERMINIST: Then what we saw before in relation to souls turns out to be true for the will as well: As soon as you accept this first premise, it follows that there is no freedom at all. Even the will has no privileged status—it is not free at all!

LIBERTARIAN: Are you suggesting, then, that will is only a sort of feeling, which is predetermined, and that the feeling of freedom that accompanies it is nothing but an illusion?

DETERMINIST: Absolutely! First, the formation of our present desires, as we have just seen, was predetermined a long time ago, and so there is no freedom in their formation.

Second, these desires and their "possessors," if we may call ourselves that, lack all freedom to influence the future world, since all future states of the world—in a moment, in a year, in a thousand years—were absolutely predetermined from the very beginning of time.

LIBERTARIAN: These are totally intolerable conclusions! If there is no free will and no genuine freedom, then life has lost its savor. Then, at least from a moral standpoint, we must adopt the other possibility.

DETERMINIST: And what is that?

2

Antideterminism and the Will

LIBERTARIAN: If that is how things are, then it would be better to abandon our first premise, because the very acceptance of that premise has predetermined our conclusion: that everything is predetermined.

DETERMINIST: Are you referring to the premise about causality? To the claim that causality applies to everything?

LIBERTARIAN: Precisely. Perhaps this claim is tolerable with respect to the material components of the world, but not its immaterial components, such as desires, souls, and the like.

But since you prefer one law for everything, let's assume the opposite of our original premise, and say that there are no laws of causality, or that nothing in the universe obeys such laws. Then you will have to concede that your determinism will vanish.

DETERMINIST: This I must admit. Shall we dare to follow Hume and speculate that there is no such thing as "causal relations," and that neither the universe as a whole nor any of its parts operates according to the laws of causality?

LIBERTARIAN: Yes, let's do that.

DETERMINIST: In other words, there is nothing—and I stress *nothing*—that can constitute a cause or an effect?

LIBERTARIAN: For the sake of the argument, let's assume that this is so, in order to show the theoretical possibility of free will. Let's call this hypothesis "antideterminism," as it is the antithesis of your determinism.

DETERMINIST: Okay. But according to this premise, the will can't be a cause, for there are no causes or effects. So if you want to raise your hand in a moment, it's impossible for your will to bring it about, since the will cannot be the cause of any state of affairs. You must agree that this is a very strange sort of will . . .

LIBERTARIAN: Oh, there's a bit of a problem here . . .

DETERMINIST: ''A bit of a problem?'' What's the use of ''free will'' if it can't have any influence on anything, and if even the strongest desire can't be carried out, except by chance?

Is there any point in assuming such a ''will'' if it can't ever play any role?

LIBERTARIAN: Okay, okay—it really is a serious problem.

DETERMINIST: And here is another problem that's even more serious: According to your antideterminism, not only are desires not a cause of anything, but nothing is the cause of desires, as nothing is determined or caused by anything else.

LIBERTARIAN: And what of it?

DETERMINIST: It turns out, then, that desires are entirely random, not dependent on and not connected with any states of affairs in the world, not even to our mental state at the previous moment. Let's assume, for example, that I'm looking at a pretty flower. According to antideterminism it would not be possible for this event to be a cause of my desire to see it again, for the sight of a flower cannot serve as a cause.

LIBERTARIAN: This difficulty is becoming rather serious. It turns out that antideterminism precludes the possibility of free will.

DETERMINIST: Just like determinism, antideterminism is also fatal to the possibility of free will. If we assume that determinism is true, then there is no freedom, and the will turns out to be something whose existence and function are predetermined.

If, on the other hand, we assume the truth of antideterminism, then it is impossible for the will to fulfill any function, and so it becomes meaningless. Thus when we return some freedom to the system, the will itself dissolves into randomness.

If there is will, there is no freedom. If there is freedom, there is no will.

LIBERTARIAN: In that case, only one alternative remains . . .

3

Semideterminism and the Will

DETERMINIST: Another possibility? One or the other—either determinism is true, or else its negation, antideterminism, is true.

LIBERTARIAN: There's a third possibility—"semideterminism."

DETERMINIST: This is the first time I've heard of such a theory. What does it mean?

LIBERTARIAN: Determinism follows from the premise that everything operates only in accordance with the laws of causality; antideterminism follows from the premise that nothing is a cause or an effect. The truth is probably somewhere in the middle, between the two extremes. Let's assume that causality does apply to the universe, but only partially.

DETERMINIST: I must admit that this is a theoretical possibility. But in order for it to have any meaning you must explain what you mean by it.

LIBERTARIAN: I mean that the laws of causality do not apply absolutely, but only partially.

DETERMINIST: But what do you mean by "partially?" Do you mean "partialness" in relation to time or in relation to different parts of the world? Or do you perhaps have some other sense in mind?

LIBERTARIAN: It's all the same to me. Let's assume that it's in relation to time—that causality doesn't always apply.

DETERMINIST: You mean that sometimes the whole world operates according to the laws of causality whereas at other times it does not?

LIBERTARIAN: That's right.

DETERMINIST: Okay, then let's assume that now, at this very moment, the laws of causality apply fully. Then my present actions and desires are absolutely determined by the previous state of the world. Does it make any difference how long the universe has been operating according to causality—a million years, one year, a single minute? No, since in any case my present desires and actions were determined by some previous events, so they don't manifest any genuine freedom.

Am I right in claiming this?

LIBERTARIAN: It seems right to me.

DETERMINIST: Fine, and now let's assume the opposite: that there are no causes and effects at this moment. Then my will at this time is absolutely random, as nothing in the present can be the effect of anything else. Moreover, my present desires can't be the cause of anything else, and so they are stripped of all meaning.

In any case, if we assume that the universe operates at certain times according to causality and at other times not, it is impossible for a particular action to influence future events. For a few moments of randomness in the chain of causes and effects will cancel any possibility of influence beyond this break in the chain. It's like holding a long rope that's cut at some point—no matter how hard I struggle to pull it, the other end will not budge.

LIBERTARIAN: It's clear to me now that our concept of partialness can't be time-related. But how about a partition of the universe into two classes of entities? Let's suppose there are two sorts of objects: those operating according to the laws of causality, and those that are not subject to these laws.

DETERMINIST: In such a case there would be an absolute dichotomy between the two parts. For there could not be any causal relation between those things that can be causes and effects and those things that are incapable of being causes and effects.

But then where would you put the will? If you assign the will to that part of the universe that is not subject to the laws of causality, then it is random, senseless, and useless.

If, on the other hand, you assign the will to the part that is subject to these laws, then one's desires will influence and be influenced by only the part of the universe that also operates according to these laws. Hence, in those parts of the universe there will exist a strict determinism just like the one I argued for at the beginning of this discussion. Once again there will be no room for freedom—everything will be determined in advance.

LIBERTARIAN: Is there perhaps another way to formulate our concept of partialness? Is it perhaps possible to formulate a statistical version of causation, where some effects are caused only with a certain probability? For example, let's say that for each cause there are several possible effects, each with a certain probability.

DETERMINIST: There have been some attempts recently to provide scientific backing for such a suggestion—I am referring to a particular interpretation of quantum mechanics. But do you really believe that a statistical approach will give meaning to the notion of free will?

For my part, I believe that any formulation of semideterminism is, in the final analysis, an incoherent mixture of randomness and determinism. And as we have already seen, mixtures of causation and coincidence are no less fatal to the notion of free will than causation or coincidence alone.

4

"Socratic" Dialogue on Free Will

I heard the following discussion on a warm summer's day. At dawn, when Meridas, Lysias, and I left the council building and walked toward the city gates, we suddenly encountered Lucas and Socrates, who were walking more slowly. They seemed to be deep in an ardent discussion. After exchanging greetings, we asked them to continue their discussion and permit us to listen, as we were walking in the same direction. This is what we heard:

LUCAS: And I also heard you've been telling people that there is no free will.

SOCRATES: Then you heard correctly.

LUCAS: If you're referring to the barbarians who are subordinate to their kings, I'll be happy to agree with you. But do you claim that citizens of city-states like Athens, such as ourselves, also lack free will?

SOCRATES: Well, I make no specific claims about it. For how could I distinguish possessors of free will, when I claim that there is no possibility that such a thing could exist? And what could be the purpose of ascribing freedom to something which by its very nature cannot be free?

LUCAS: But really, Socrates, haven't you heard our experienced politicians lecturing on the difference between Athenians and barbarians? For we in Athens are free men, and this distinguishes us from the Persians and other barbarians. In Persia, for example, everyone must subdue his will to the king's will; whereas here, in Athens, every one of us—and at least with respect to myself I can be certain of this—has his own private free will. And every one of us may act according to his desires, as long as he does not harm others or disobey the law.

SOCRATES: If that's your stand, then you shouldn't find it difficult to explain what you say "free will" is.

LUCAS: It will indeed be easy: My free will is my desire to do whatever occurs to me, for my own benefit, and in the way I prefer.

SOCRATES: Indeed, Lucas? Are you distinguishing between what occurs to you to do and your desires?

LUCAS: Not at all. Of course what occurs to me to do for myself is identical with my desires.

SOCRATES: And what is the relation between your desires and your will? Is there anything you desire but do not want? Or anything you want without desiring it?

LUCAS: Are you making fun of me so early in the morning? It's obvious that what one wants is what one desires to have, and vice versa. Wanting and desiring are synonyms.

SOCRATES: On the contrary, Lucas, you are the one who is making fun of me. For I asked you what will is, or what free will is, and you answered that will is desiring and desiring is will. How can that tell me anything new about will?

LUCAS: I didn't mean to make fun of you, Socrates. But since I know your subtle ways of argument, I suspect that if I keep on trying to define "will" I might end up making a laughingstock of myself. So perhaps you will have mercy on me, and on all of us, and tell us your own ideas about the will. For if you are sincere you will have to admit that sometimes you feel there is something you want.

SOCRATES: You want me to be sincere, Lucas. If so, I must admit that I feel as though I want many things. But when I examine these feelings philosophically, they seem to be like dreams. In my dreams I imagine people and other objects, yet when I wake up I realize that these "objects" were not real.

It seems to me that the same is true of my feeling of will. I have a feeling of "free will," and this feeling deceives me into believing that "free will" exists, just as my dreams deceive me into believing in the existence of the people and objects I see in them.

LUCAS: It seems to me, Socrates, that in your effort to show that the question is unanswerable, you have actually answered it. For you have explained that the will is a kind of feeling or activity of the soul! And this is exactly what I tried to tell you before.

Then Socrates turned to us and said: You see how sly our friend Lucas is. He has just put his words into my mouth, and in a moment he will accuse me of being petty and of trying to make fun of him the way he made fun of me before.

LUCAS: What makes you think that, Socrates?

SOCRATES: You claim that I answered the question "What is the will?" by saying that "the will" is "the feeling of will." Do you really expect me not to notice that this is the same sort of circular answer as your own previous definition? Actually I don't have any answer to the question, as I really don't know what will, or free will, is.

But perhaps we can make some progress if you try to answer the following questions: Do you think that the will is like a prisoner? Or must it be free?

LUCAS: What do you mean by that?

SOCRATES: What I mean is: Can a person desire anything he wants to desire? Or is the will restricted to desiring certain specific things?

LUCAS: I already told you at the beginning of our discussion that what makes us the possessors of free will is exactly what distinguishes us from the Persians. They are commanded to desire and do whatever their king wants, and so they do not have free will. From this I conclude that a will which is not free is not worthy of being called a will at all.

SOCRATES: That is a fine conclusion, which should be kept in mind. A will that is not free is not a genuine will. But now answer this: Are you not born of woman?

LUCAS: Naturally.

SOCRATES: And of what is your will born?

LUCAS: Your question is very strange, Socrates—it came into the world with me.

SOCRATES: And before you were born, did your will already exist?

LUCAS: Of course my will could not have existed before I did, since it is defined as *my* will.

SOCRATES: In that case, am I justified in saying that your will came into the world at exactly the same moment that you did?

LUCAS: Exactly. Moreover, since it was I who created it and brought it into the world, it could not have come into existence before me.

SOCRATES: And could a person possibly do anything before he was born?

LUCAS: How could something that does not exist do anything?

SOCRATES: Then it isn't possible for him to cause anything.

LUCAS: Obviously, since he doesn't exist. What are you driving at?

SOCRATES: There are two things I don't understand: First, how could you have brought your will into the world with you at the moment of your birth? And second, how could you have created it? When could you have managed to do this?

LUCAS: What I meant is that I developed it just after I was born, and not before that.

SOCRATES: Then let me ask you: Why did you do this?

LUCAS: "Why"? What do you mean by that?

SOCRATES: You are saying that you developed your will yourself. Then did you have any will before you did this?

LUCAS: Apparently not.

SOCRATES: It would seem, then, that when you constructed your original will, you did not do this because you wanted to, as at that point you did not have any will to order its construction!

LUCAS: That's how it seems.

SOCRATES: But then what happened before you had any will? Did you want to construct your original will to be strong or weak or to have some other features?

LUCAS: Before I had a will I didn't want anything.

SOCRATES: Surely you must have heard the saying that "if something is not done out of will it is done out of compulsion." And so if you did not yet have any will, then . . .

At this point Lucas raised his hands in surrender, and interrupted Socrates in the middle of his speech.

LUCAS: Enough, Socrates, I must admit that the lesson of this is that I created my will out of compulsion and total necessity. And now, to tell the truth, I feel that my will has become passive and I am compelled to answer your question as you want, since you leave me no other choice.

SOCRATES: And this will of yours, isn't it true that everything it wants was predetermined by its original nature? And since we've agreed that it was necessarily constructed to have the specific features that it has, then isn't it also necessary that in each specific situation it should desire very specific things? And if you agree to this, we can say about you what you previously said about the Persians: that you are not free at all, as your predetermined will compels you to want what you want.

LUCAS: That's true. But can we perhaps consider the possibility that my original will created a new, freer will some time later?

SOCRATES: And if it really did this, could it have done otherwise? Could it have acted against its own nature?

LUCAS: It seems not.

SOCRATES: In other words, even your second will, as you call it, was not chosen freely by you, but was forced upon you. And the same is true of the third and the fourth and all their descendants—they can never be free if they originated from your initial will, which itself was never free.

Why don't you answer me? Have you stopped desiring our conversation?

LUCAS: You're right, Socrates.

SOCRATES: But let's suppose you have a will that came from some other source. Can it be said to be free, precisely because it was imposed on you from the outside?

LUCAS: That would verge on the absurd. But what should we conclude, Socrates—that there is no will at all? Don't you often say that you want something?

SOCRATES: We must realize that what we call our "will" is forced upon us, and it compels us to want only according to it. And if we are not free to want what we want, then how can we be free? Yet if we agree with what you said before—that an unfree will is not a will at all—then we have only an illusory feeling of will.

In the meantime the sun had reached its zenith. Having been walking the whole time, we had reached a grove near the stream.

We all felt that the discussion was over, as we couldn't see any way to disprove Socrates' arguments. So we all sat down on the shady grass to rest for a while before taking a swim. Only Lucas continued to pace back and forth, and finally he addressed Socrates again.

LUCAS: Your argument is indeed very cogent. Yet I am looking for some way of refuting it, as my desire to do so remains very strong. And when I contemplate this desire of mine, I feel once again that my will is free! And again I don't know what to rely on—the logic of your reasoning, or my own feelings.

But Socrates, who was lying on the grass, didn't answer: he was asleep. And it seemed as if we were all sleeping until young Lysias jumped up and exclaimed: "Eureka! I think I've found a flaw in Socrates' argument!" When we asked him what he had thought of, he said we should wait until Socrates woke up, as it would be a pity to disturb him. But Socrates jumped up as if bitten by a snake.

SOCRATES: Speak. I am awake.

LYSIAS: Oh, forgive me, Socrates. I didn't mean to disturb you.

SOCRATES: My dear boy, I wouldn't have forgiven you if you hadn't woken me. Now let's hear what you have to say.

LYSIAS: I thought that if you proved that there is no free will, then at the same time you proved that there isn't any world either.

We were all dumbfounded by this bizarre claim. It seemed to me that even Socrates was a bit puzzled, and he was quiet for a moment before responding.

SOCRATES: What did you say?

LYSIAS: I meant that by the same reasoning you could also deduce the fantastic conclusion that there is no world!

SOCRATES: Would you please explain these strange remarks?

LYSIAS: I claim that when you just now denied the existence of free will, your argument was not based on showing an internal inconsistency between the concepts of freedom and will. Rather, you claimed that free will doesn't exist because there's no way it could have come about.

SOCRATES: That's true.

LYSIAS: Then your actual argument was that free will doesn't exist because there is no way that genuine freedom could be created.

SOCRATES: And what's wrong with that?

LYSIAS: But didn't you once meet Parmenides, who says "What there is exists and the nothing does not exist"?

SOCRATES: I did.

LYSIAS: And do you believe that Parmenides was right in claiming that what there is cannot be created from nothing?

SOCRATES: It seems to me that he was.

LYSIAS: Then you'll surely also agree that if what there is had a beginning, it could not have been created from what there is, because it didn't exist before it was created.

SOCRATES: Yes, that seems right to me.

LYSIAS: Yet what there is does exist, doesn't it?

SOCRATES: Certainly.

LYSIAS: Then kindly tell us how it was created.

SOCRATES: I can't explain it. The creation of the world is beyond my comprehension.

LYSIAS: Yet you don't deny its existence.

SOCRATES: No, I don't.

LYSIAS: Then why do you deny the existence of the will? Before, in your discussion with Lucas about free will, you claimed that there isn't any such thing because it's impossible to explain how it came into being. But if you want to be consistent, then the same logic dictates that the world does not exist, since there is no way of showing how and from what it could have been created. But since you don't say that, and you don't deny that the world exists, you must also admit that free will exists!

At this point we all broke out in exclamations of admiration for the way Lysias had succeeded in steering the conversation.

It had been a long time since any of us had heard someone argue with Socrates as an equal. Even Socrates heaped praises on our young friend.

And then Lucas asked: So what do you say, Socrates: Is there free will or isn't there?

SOCRATES: I don't believe there is.

LYSIAS: But why? Haven't you agreed that the status of the will is the same as that of the world?

SOCRATES: Are you asking me or telling me?

LYSIAS: I'm humbly asking for your opinion, Socrates.

SOCRATES: I very much admire your way of investigating the issue, but I still believe that the matter is far from being solved.

LYSIAS: Perhaps, but I don't see what else there is to say about it.

*

On our way back we asked Socrates to choose one of us as his conversational partner, because we were very keen to find out whether Socrates could defend his thesis of the impossibility of free will in the face of Lysias' argument.

SOCRATES: I suggest Lysias himself. A person who asks so well should also be able to answer well.

LYSIAS: I will gladly answer your questions, Socrates, if you agree to discuss my analogy between the world and the will.

SOCRATES: Can you, Lysias, and all the rest of you as well, turn around and see Mt. Hagliasossos rising up at the edge of the plain?

LYSIAS: Even old people with weak eyes can see that mountain.

We continued walking in silence for a few moments until Socrates spoke again.

SOCRATES: Well, Lysias, is the mountain still there?

LYSIAS (laughing): Strange as it may seem, the mountain hasn't run away yet, in spite of your presence in the vicinity.

SOCRATES: And what do you think: Is it likely to disappear to-night?

LYSIAS: Why do you suspect that the mountain will disappear? It has probably been there since the dawn of creation!
   That's the nature of mountains, Socrates. They stay where they are, as long as nothing disturbs their rest.

SOCRATES: Would you say that this is the nature of all material things, or only of mountains?

LYSIAS: Every material thing remains in its place and in its state, unless it is disturbed by something else.

SOCRATES: And is Mt. Hagliasossos, which you are looking at now, the same mountain that was standing there five minutes ago?

LYSIAS: Of course, since nothing has changed in the meantime. But what connection is there between the will and the mountain?

SOCRATES: I'll get to it in a moment. Shall we conclude, then, that material objects of all types tend to remain as they are and retain the same features, as long as they are not disturbed by an external force?

LYSIAS: I agree wholeheartedly.

SOCRATES: Now, what about the will? Shall we say about it what we said about the mountain?

LYSIAS: What a strange comparison!

SOCRATES: Let's consider it anyway. Listen carefully: Let's assume that a certain person, say Rufus, comes into the world equipped with free will.

LYSIAS: But then, as you said before, we would have to explain how his will was created.

SOCRATES: Let's leave that problem aside for the moment, Lysias, as you've shown us that there are things whose existence we recognize even though we don't understand how they could have been created. Let's assume now that even though we don't know where his will came from, this Rufus came into the world blessed with free will. Is this clear?

LYSIAS: Quite clear.

SOCRATES: And now several years have passed, and Lysias and Socrates meet this Rufus and his will again—just as they contemplated the mountain before at two different moments.

LYSIAS: Okay.

SOCRATES: And now let's talk to Rufus' will and ask it: "O will of Rufus, are you the selfsame one as Rufus' will of some years ago? Or did another will enter Rufus and take up residence there?"

LYSIAS: I don't know how it would answer.

SOCRATES: Let's assume it would answer something like what the mountain would answer—that it's the very same will of the very same person.

LYSIAS: I'm willing to assume that.

SOCRATES: And now we ask it: "O will of Rufus, have you retained the same features that you had before?" And the will answers thus: "Since I'm still the same will, at least most of the features that I had before have been retained. This means, for instance, that if some years ago I didn't care what people think, then I'm still the same now, and the same is true for the other features that can be attributed to the will."

What do you think, Lysias? Isn't it possible that it might answer this way?

LYSIAS: It's certainly possible.

SOCRATES: Thus we've learned from its answers that the same thing that occurred with the mountain has occurred with the will as well. Except for minor changes, both of them have remained the same.

LYSIAS: That's right.

SOCRATES: And even if Rufus' will reports that it has undergone some changes, surely it will ascribe them to the intervention of factors and circumstances that have affected it, just as the mountain could also be affected by rain, wind, earthquakes, and other external forces.

LYSIAS: Yes, that's what it would say.

SOCRATES: And now, listen carefully, for Socrates and Lysias are going to ask Rufus' will a hard question: "O will of Rufus, do the features you've retained include the feature of freedom? That is, can you still be called a 'free will'?''

What do you think, Lysias? How will it answer now?

LYSIAS: You've asked it a difficult question this time, and I don't know how it will answer.

SOCRATES: Well, there are only two possibilities. Suppose it answers in the negative and says that it is no longer free, since this feature cannot be retained in the long range. It is clear that such an answer would end our discussion.

LYSIAS: Yet it could also answer: ''Yes, I'm the same as I was in this respect as well—I'm still a free will.'' Then what would we ask it next?

SOCRATES: Then we'd ask it why it retained this feature. If it claims that it is its nature to do so, just as it is the nature of mountains to retain their basic features, then we'll laugh and say: If you weren't free to maintain your freedom, but its preservation was forced upon you from the outset, then you aren't free at all!

LYSIAS: And what if it says that the preservation of its freedom was not the result of compulsion but occurred by chance?

SOCRATES: Then we'll laugh even louder—for if freedom came to it without being willed in advance, then it certainly isn't real freedom.

By now we were all convinced that this was the end of the discussion, but then Merides joined in.

MERIDES: But still, Socrates, in spite of your clever twists, I'm certain that I at least have free will.

SOCRATES: And where did this free will come from, Merides? Surely you didn't make it yourself, since you couldn't want to make it before you had it.

MERIDES: No, Socrates, I didn't make it, and it doesn't matter to me in the least where it came from. We can simply assume that one day it just entered me and that's that.

SOCRATES: So there was this free will roaming around the world, and one day it encountered Merides and settled in him?

MERIDES: As simple as that.

SOCRATES: And if you didn't have this free will of yours, then you wouldn't be free?

MERIDES: Right.

SOCRATES: Then it's your free will that gives you freedom?

MERIDES: Yes.

SOCRATES: And are you proud of being the owner of a free will? Is it precious to you?

MERIDES: More precious than diamonds.

SOCRATES: In that case, there is no more miserable person than Merides in the entire world.

MERIDES: Why? It is those who have no free will who are miserable, while those who possess it are happy to have it.

SOCRATES: Poor Merides, the most miserable of all. For you are miserable precisely because your will is free.

MERIDES: You're speaking utter nonsense, Socrates.

SOCRATES: For Merides is going around in great fear, just because his will is free.

MERIDES: Great Zeus! Are you trying to frighten me?

SOCRATES: For certainly Merides is going around and thinking, "Just as my free will entered me without warning, perhaps it will just as suddenly leave me and flee."

MERIDES: Nonsense! Who ever heard of a will abandoning its owner?

SOCRATES: Haven't we established that it's free? Then why isn't it free to leave?

MERIDES: But how could it leave?

SOCRATES: The same way it entered! Just like a bird perching on a flower—if it senses that the flower has wilted, it will certainly take flight again, seeking a nicer flower than Merides to perch on.

MERIDES: In my opinion, as soon as a free will has established itself within a person, it cannot leave.

SOCRATES: But isn't it at least free to want to leave?

MERIDES: That I don't know. But let's assume that it's a law of nature that a will can on no account leave its owner.

SOCRATES: But as it's free, then it surely must follow that it is free to want to leave?

MERIDES: Perhaps.

SOCRATES: Then does this free will reside in Merides like a bird whose wings have been caught in a flower?

MERIDES: Possibly.

SOCRATES: It wants to fly but it cannot?

MERIDES: Perhaps.

SOCRATES: Mightn't the free will become very angry to have its former freedom of movement taken away?

MERIDES: Perhaps.

SOCRATES: And perhaps, just as the bird would try to tear and destroy the wilted flower in which it was trapped, mightn't the free will do the same to Merides, who is trapping it?

MERIDES: What do you mean?

SOCRATES: Well, it has many options. It can desire things that are quite harmful to Merides—that he should eat bad food and keep company with worthless people, that he should speak without thinking and do many other bad things.

MERIDES: On no account would I do any of these things.

SOCRATES: Why not?

MERIDES: Obviously I wouldn't want to harm myself.

SOCRATES: That's what you think now. But when your will wants you to want something, can you possibly avoid desiring it?
  Does Merides have a multitude of wills within himself?

MERIDES: Well, then, Socrates, you've convinced me. I give up my free will.

SOCRATES: You don't want it any more?

MERIDES: No.

SOCRATES: Then you never had it at all.

Further Reading for Part III

Plato

The dialogue "Gorgias" is not easy reading, but it handsomely repays any effort invested in it. Socrates' view is that all men want one and only one thing: "the good." It is logically impossible to want the bad. If it seems to us that someone is trying to attain something bad, it must be because that person is confused between good and bad; he does not know how to recognize the good. In Socrates' view, people are not free to decide what to want; rather, their will directs them to one thing: "the good." In other words, people are not free to determine their own desires. This paradoxical thesis is especially stressed in Socrates' discussion with Paulus. The dialogue "Gorgias" may be found in *The Dialogues of Plato*, trans. B. Jowett, New York, 1973.

Nietzsche

Determinism is discussed in the last chapter of his book *The Will to Power*, Vol. II. Nietzsche goes beyond the deterministic claim that all future events were determined long ago. He claims, in the words of Ecclesiastes, that "only that shall happen which has happened," and insists on the "eternal recurrence" of the entire history of the universe. The classic translation of this work is that of Walter Kaufmann, New York, 1968.

General Discussion

•Taylor's book *Metaphysics* includes a discussion of freedom, determinism, and fatalism. The presentation of the topic is very lucid and contains a fascinating story about a boy called "Osmo" who reads the story of his life before the events have actually taken place. *Metaphysics* was published by Prentice-Hall in 1974.

117

Glossary

A priori or **apriori**—Prior to experience: innate to the mind.

Determinism—The doctrine that everything that happens, including human behavior, is compelled to happen by a necessary chain of causation from the beginning of time.

Dichotomy—A sharp division; the partition of something into two mutually exclusive classes.

Dualism—(from *duo*, two) The doctrine that mind and matter, or soul and body, exist as independent entities.

Empiricism—The theory that regards experience and observation as the only sources of knowledge. (Opposed to rationalism, q.v.)

Epistemology—Theories of the grounds of knowledge.

Idealism (empirical)—The theory that objects of external perception consist of ideas in the perceiving mind.

Materialism—The doctrine that nothing exists except matter and its transformation.

Metaphysics—(literally, above physics) The philosophy dealing with the first principles of all things.

Rationalism—The theory that regards reason, rather than experience, as the foundation of knowledge. (Opposed to empiricism, q.v.)

Index